W9-BIH-694

The American Political System

A Background Book on Democratic Procedure

The American Political System

A Background Book on Democratic Procedure

by ROBERT A. LISTON

with an editorial by Norman Cousins

Parents' Magazine Press • New York

Each Background Book is concerned with the broad spectrum of people, places, and events affecting the national and international scene. Written simply and clearly, the books in the series will engage the minds and interests of people living in a world of great change.

To Eddie Ballard
. . . Beta

Contents

Acknowledgments

The author and publishers gratefully acknowledge permission to quote from the following copyrighted materials (the pages on which the quotations appear are indicated in the *Notes*, which begin on page 225):

The Deadlock of Democracy: Four Party Politics in America by James MacGregor Burns, published by Prentice-Hall, Inc. Copyright © 1963 by James MacGregor Burns.

Majority Rule and Minority Rights by Henry Steele Commager, published by Oxford University Press.

The Legislative Process in Congress by George B. Galloway. Copyright © 1953 by Thomas Y. Crowell Company, Inc. Reprinted with the permission of the publisher.

The Selling of the President 1968 by Joe McGinniss, published by Trident Press, division of Simon & Schuster, Inc. Copyright © 1969 by Joemac, Incorporated.

The Case for Optimism

Publisher's note: What follows is not the usual preface to a book. It is an editorial from the *Saturday Review** of November 20, 1971 — the last one Norman Cousins, editor of *Saturday Review* from 1940 to 1971, wrote before his "Final Report to the Readers" on November 27th. While it makes no direct reference to *The American Political System* and, in fact, Mr. Cousins had not read Robert Liston's book, its tone and content seemed to fit Mr. Liston's thesis so well that we asked for, and received, Mr. Cousins' permission to use it and for this we are grateful.

Recently, in Vancouver, British Columbia, I was asked whether I was optimistic about life in the United States. The questioner then recited a long list of minuses: the Vietnam War, the Amchitka nuclear test, the Mylai slaughter, deteriorating conditions in American cities, racial unrest, fierce poverty at a time of mammoth national income, deepening military influence in the nation's political, economic, and social affairs, and the general mood of violence in the life-style of the people.

I found myself in a position I had been in a number of times over the years, in such places as India, Pakistan, Nigeria, the Cameroons, Poland, Czechoslovakia, and the Soviet Union. People would ask questions in a way that indicated they expected a starkly negative reply. But I would find my answers running counter to their expectations. There is nothing like a vantage point outside the U.S. for instant perspective. It isn't so much that you feel the need to defend your country against outside criticism. What happens is that you realize

people in other countries tend to reach distorted conclusions about the U.S., and you feel obligated to provide what
you believe is a full and balanced appraisal.

One advantage of such an encounter is that you find your
own views being put to the test. Just in the act of drawing up
a balance sheet, you are apt to discover you are more optimistic than you realized. And this is what happened in Vancouver.
As I attempted to respond to the specific points raised by my
questioner, I found it necessary to deal with both pluses and
minuses. Even on Vietnam, one could cite a substantial change
from the situation of two years ago. A date for final with-
drawal has not been set, but more than two-thirds of our troops
have already left. American casualties have sharply decreased.
This is not good enough, but at least we are no longer attempting to cope with the tragedy of Vietnam by compounding it.
Two years ago, the public debate was over the pace of the
escalation; today it is over the pace of de-escalation. Nothing
is more predictable than the fact that for at least the next
decade the American people in general and American historians in particular will be intensively combing over the mistakes
that led us into the war and then prolonged it. This is all to
the good.

Perhaps more important than anything else about Vietnam,
however, is that it has come to represent a great dividing line
in American history. The notion no longer holds that a U.S.
President has a blank check in the field of foreign policy.
There has been a fundamental change in the kinds of commitments that will be made by the President or by the military
under him. U.S. foreign policy may not yet be in a state of
ideal balance, but some of the balancing factors have at last
come into play.

What has brought about the change? A multiplicity of factors, chief among which has been a widespread disillusion with
the war and with all the attempts of government to make it
seem to be something it was not. In a more general sense, what
happened was that all the mechanisms of public opinion began
to have a direct effect on the Vietnam War. The nation's youth
spoke and acted, sometimes with fury but always with moral
fervor. The fury might be deplored but the fervor could not

be denied. Priests, nuns, ministers, and rabbis not only sanc-
tioned anti-war protests but were in the front ranks. Businessmen formed a national organization to oppose the war. Newspaper and television reporters, editorial writers, and commentators kept coming up with facts that contradicted the accounts
of government and made it increasingly difficult for officialdom
to manipulate public opinion. The system was working.

What do we mean when we say that? No one—certainly not
the framers of the U.S. Constitution—promised a system that
could unfailingly produce wisdom and justice. What was promised and provided was a system that gave the people a chance
to correct or dismiss the error-makers and trouble-makers.
Men of poor judgment—indeed, knaves and scoundrels—
might come to public office and they might inflict damage on
the society; but they would be foolish to think that they
would not encounter resistance or even be tossed out on their
ears. What is truly significant about Americans in office is not
their day-to-day power but their ultimate powerlessness. Too
many people are looking over their shoulders and they have
to run too many gauntlets for them to be immune or inac-
cessible.

This process of public monitoring, with all its flux and frus-
trations, is in evidence not just on the Vietnam War but on
many of the other problems mentioned by the Vancouver
questioner. The nuclear test at Amchitka was rammed
through. The problem here was not that the government was
unreceptive to public opinion but that not enough leaders of
public opinion ever really got into this act. At least, the government was never made to feel that it was dealing with a
powerful force, as happened almost a decade ago during the
fight over a limited nuclear test ban. But public opinion was
stronger on Cannikin II than it was on Cannikin I. And the
mounting protests in Canada and Japan over the arrogance of
the United States in ignoring the appeals of others who might
be affected will make the next test outside the continental
United States that much more difficult.

As for Mylai, one fact that has been generally overlooked in
the clamorous debate over the responsibility for the outrages
is that this is the first time a nation has openly tried members

of its own military for brutality or atrocities. The fact that men on the firing line rather than in the higher echelons were tried may be deplored and debated, but this does not set aside the historic significance of the trials.

Meanwhile, the unilateral destruction of the stockpiles of bacteriological weapons by the United States represents the first instance of any importance in which weapons have been renounced and eliminated rather than just limited. And, considering the strong case made by the military for the manufacture of such weapons, the President's decision to destroy the stockpiles should not be undervalued.

Similarly, it is difficult to overestimate the historic significance of the new U.S. policy on China. Few factors affecting the peace of the world carry more weight than the relationship of China to the West.

Returning to the other major American problems listed by my questioner in Vancouver—problems of poverty, human rights, environmental deterioration, the collapse of the cities, and all the rest—no one knows whether enough progress can be made in time to prevent a spiraling downturn in our society. But the nation has a substantial asset today for attempting to meet these problems. I refer to the nation's youth. The present generation of young Americans serves as reason enough for optimism over the American future, even if all other reasons were lacking. Taken as a whole, the youth of America today are probably more mindful of the seriousness of the nation's problems than any previous generation of Americans. They are asking hard questions and are insisting on honest answers.

They are tough-minded but tenderhearted. They cannot be pushed around—intellectually, socially, or politically. They can smell humbug or hypocrisy a mile away. They can't be fobbed off with slick formulations, and they don't lend themselves to manipulation—whether by government, teachers, parents, or even their own peers. They place proper value on human feelings as well as on human needs. They will literally turn the world upside down to combat cruelty or injustice. They have no particular fondness for organizations as such, but they like to work closely together so long as things don't become too formal or institutionalized. Above all, they shun artificiality and ostentation. They see no reason for disguising or changing the natural look of things. They are perhaps more a puzzlement to their parents than they would have been to their great-grandmothers who baked their own bread, knitted socks and sweaters, loved folk songs, and thought that fancy makeup actually detracted from the good looks of young girls. The youth of the nation are rediscovering religion, not so much as worship but as a way of life. They are not afraid to go all the way in behalf of a moral or spiritual conviction and are literally determined to bet their lives on what they consider to be a moral principle.

They have no difficulty in recognizing the dominant challenge of the time, which is to comprehend the meaning of human oneness as well as to be able to accept allegiance to the family of man. They know that war, in the context of weapons of absolute destruction, has become total insanity, and they are unimpressed with the tradition that says there is no other way.

Have we nothing critical to say about youth? We are troubled that in their determination to see things in a new light they tend to cut themselves off from history. This makes the job of building a better world infinitely harder and more protracted than it need be. We are troubled, too, by the notion that the use of hard language is a blow for liberation. These are artificialities quite as pronounced as some of the affectations youth properly condemn in the older generation. But the dominant thrust of youth is toward sanity and integrity, whatever the incongruities.

Nor are we giving up on the older generation. Americans can bring about the great changes that are needed in their own country and in the world because they are attuned to change historically. They don't have to develop new political or philosophical reflexes before they can face up to their needs.

There is hope, then, in a plastic definition of Americans. The case for optimism goes beyond the recognition of a divine itch or the sudden notion that there is an extra minute before midnight. The American experiment has succeeded in a way that Madison and Hamilton never dared dream it would. Its essential claim—that nothing is more important than individual man—has met the test and has been echoed on every continent. The individual man has come into his own. Thinking, feeling, musing, complaining, fending, creating, building, evading, desiring, he has become more important to the operators of his governments than ever before. The question, therefore, is not whether man is capable of prolonging and ennobling his stay on earth. The question is whether he recognizes his prime power—and also his duty—for accomplishing that purpose.

Having said this, I am quite prepared to set it all aside for the single most important argument in favor of optimism. Optimism supplies the basic energy of civilization. Optimism doesn't wait on facts. It deals with prospects. Pessimism is a waste of time.   —N.C.

Introduction

I SHALL BEGIN by saying what this book is *not*. It is *not* a history of either the United States or of American political development. There will be some discussion of past events, but only as a means of explaining the present and, perhaps, guiding the future.

I admit to relinquishing the history somewhat reluctantly. I have written a few times and said many times that I believe much of our problem in America today is that we are such poor history students. "Those who cannot remember the past," wrote philosopher George Santayana, "are condemned to repeat it." And so, I think, Americans, unaware of our past, repeat mistakes rather than learn from them.

There is no shortage of examples. The adherents of the peace movement today are, it may be hoped, aware that every war in American history, except World War II, was accompanied by protests, demonstrations, denouncements, and rioting in the name of peace. Our forefathers were more vigorous perhaps in protesting the War of 1812, the Mexican War, the Civil War, and our imperialist interventions in the Pacific and Caribbean than their progeny are today. The gunning down of students at Kent, Ohio and Jackson, Mississippi in recent times pales before the wholesale slaughter of strikers in the not-very-distant past. Those who denounce modern political trials might learn from the vast number of political trials that stud our history.

We Americans have either forgotten much of our past or we never knew it. I suspect the latter. Historians are somewhat at fault in this, as well as those who teach history and write history books. But society gets most of the blame. The teaching of American history is required by most state governments, but the content of the history books was carefully censored for decades by veteran and patriotic groups. The result today is a glorified notion of American history and government, which leaves us all deficient in the accurate information about our past that could illuminate the present.

But this is a digression. Reluctantly, this is not a history book.

Nor is it a primer on American government. I am assuming that you, the reader, have a basic working knowledge of American government, including such things as what Congress is, how a law is enacted, the powers of the Supreme Court, and at least some of the powers of the president and executive branch. I am assuming you are acquainted with the federal nature of our political system, and a great deal more.

I make these assumptions, quite frankly, to ease what is already a most difficult task, for I am trying to explain the American political system, how it got that way, its virtues, its problems, what could possibly be done about them, and where it may be heading.

My task is to reduce to a very small space an immense subject. I feel a bit like the first man of twenty who jam themselves into a phone booth. Every chapter in this book has been the subject of large numbers of very weighty tomes. Consider the many books in the library dealing with the presidency alone, or Congress, foreign affairs, or the Constitution.

I believe there is great need for a brief overview of the political system, one striving not for thoroughness, but for understanding of the major problems and their possible solutions. Toward this end I have omitted any lengthy discourses on history, particular social or economic problems, and those political problems which seem less pertinent to current affairs.

The result of this effort is a far cry from the usual school civics book. The Founding Fathers, as brilliant as they were, never conceived of J. Edgar Hoover, a Surgeon General, or a Pure Food and Drug Administration — to name three out of hundreds of possibilities. The Founding Fathers did conceive of a Wilbur Mills sitting in the House of Representatives holding in his capable hands nearly exclusive power over the nation's taxation. All of these people — heads of government bureaus and chairmen of congressional committees — have immense powers in the United States. They influence American life as surely as the president does. In short, I'm trying to explain where power lies in Washington and in the nation, how that power is used, and how it might be used more wisely. Part of the problem in America today is that we do not realize where power lies, let alone how to influence it. We talk about The System, but we do not know what it is or how to use it.

I will be writing a great deal about Richard M. Nixon's conduct of the presidency, but only because he happens to be the man in the White House at the moment, and I want to use recent events as illustrations whenever possible. Nothing said about President Nixon or anyone else should be construed as a personal criticism of him or them.

I am keeping my personal political opinions out of this, not because I don't relish them as much as the next man, but because we all need to look at the political system coldly, analytically, without the heat engendered by political opinion. Whether a person likes, dislikes, or is simply indifferent to Mr. Nixon, J. Edgar Hoover, Wilbur Mills, or anyone else should not influence consideration of the political system and how it operates. President Nixon, whether he is admired, denounced, or causes yawns, cannot possibly be president more than eight years. Someone else will come along. The system will remain while the men change, unless those who wish a radical change in the system are successful.

Change. There will be a lot about that subject in this book, for a person needs no particular clairvoyance to see that the American political system is undergoing many changes — and rapidly. The extent of the agitation for further changes surely indicates still more changes. At no time am I advocating a particular change. I am trying to give as best I can the various viewpoints on both the problems and the changes advocated as solutions, so as to provide the information essential to anyone who must cope with the future.

I am indebted to so many people I can't even remember them all. I'd like to mention my college professor, who is now retiring, Paul I. Miller of Hiram College in Ohio; Miss Thelma Bumbaugh, librarian of that college, who made many books available to me; and Mrs. Eleanor R. Seagraves of Washington, D.C., who provides me with so much information she ought to share the byline.

La Felicidad
Benalmadena Costa, Spain
October, 1971

1

What Is the System?

"I think giving kids the vote is a step forward, but all we can do is vote in an already faulty system."

— POLLY SPIEGEL[1]

POLLY SPIEGEL'S NATIONAL prominence, for the moment at least, rests upon the fact that she was quoted in *Time* magazine. Aged 20, from Cambridge, Massachusetts, and a student at Swarthmore College, she was among eight young people whose opinions on the subject of the eighteen-year-old vote were quoted.

No one, including the editors of *Time*, knows how typical Miss Spiegel's opinion is. Many young people may feel as she does. Or she may be the only one in the whole country to have that opinion. That is what's wrong with the "man on the street" interview as a barometer of public opinion.

6

But it is to be doubted if she is alone in that view. Too many other people—young, old, and middle-aged, black and white, workingmen and businessmen, government employees and voters, long-haired radicals and short-haired straights, wearers of hot pants and of business suits—have uttered similar denunciations of the American political system for it to be assumed that Miss Spiegel is a voice in the wilderness.

In truth, criticism of the American political system has been made so often in recent years that it has become rhetoric. Worse, the criticism has reached the point of symbolism, a sort of shorthand. A speaker or a writer nowadays simply refers to "The System" or "The Establishment." He is greeted with cheers or boos, depending upon the audience he is addressing or reaching. It is simply assumed that everyone knows what The System is, or it is left for each individual to compile his own list of evils in definition of The System. Whatever it is, it is bad and must be eliminated.

If those who wish to change The System can be dubbed revolutionaries, as many who observe and write about these matters have done, then it is a most strange revolution, for it lacks a clear-cut definition of both the problems and the solutions.

What is *The System?* What is wrong? I ask that neither in agreement nor disagreement, but simply for clarification. Obviously, no one can solve anything until the problem is stated.

The problem *can* be stated. Because so many criticisms of the American political system have been made so often in recent years it is a rather simple matter to reprise them.

Government in America is unresponsive. The nation and the people have extremely serious problems which only government, collectively representing all the people, can solve. Yet government does very little other than the half-hearted. Mostly it offers lip service to programs which never seem effective. Just a partial list of such problems would include the massive deterioration of our cities and the quality of life in them; the beggaring of large numbers of the black people living in those cities until they can react only with frustration, alienation, and desperation; the pollution of the air, water, and land; indeed the whole planet until it may not be inhabitable a generation or two from now. Another list could cite problems of education, crime and punishment, transportation, communication, joblessness, and poverty in the allegedly richest nation in the world. All of these are problems entirely of government or ones that government must play a major role in solving.

Yet the problems seem to drift along. We can finance a ride on the moon but not solve the problems attendant upon going crosstown on a bus. We can fight a war halfway around the earth, but we cannot truly make war on poverty in the nation's capital. We can loan $250 million to save the nation's largest defense contractor (Lockheed Aircraft) from the mistakes of its own mismanagement, but we cannot guarantee the safety of a citizen on his street or even in his own dwelling.

Americans have little control over government. Many citizens have a feeling of aloneness and powerlessness. It is extremely difficult for an individual — or even very large groups of people — to influence government policy or actions, be it for peace or war, higher salaries, lower taxation, more public housing, improved hospitals, pollution control, education, or a long list of other concerns. No one seems to be able to exert any observable control over the Federal Bureau of Investigation, the Central Intelligence Agency, the Joint Chiefs of Staff, the Federal Aviation Agency, the . . . the . . . the — or the local school board.

People seem to get into office, a few by election, but most by appointment, and they seem to stay there forever, untouched by public attitudes. Most people, no matter how informed and concerned, are able to do very little about what government does at any level, federal, state, or local.

America seems to have a government by governors, not by the governed. Everything is done *for* the people, but almost nothing *by* the people. President Nixon announced, in August 1971, a new economic policy to relieve unemployment, stop the inflation of prices and wages, and stabilize America's currency in relation to other nations. But, for good or ill, Mr. Nixon simply took action. The people had nothing to say about formulating the policy. They could do next to nothing about changing it. About the only responsive element to the President's change in policy was that he was reacting to rather obvious public dissatisfaction over his former policy.

The lack of control is a matter of simple arithmetic. The federal government employs nearly three million people, not counting the members of the armed forces. Of this number, precisely 537 are elected — 435 representatives to Congress, 100 senators, one president and one vice president. Of the remainder, perhaps 200,000 are appointed; that is, they serve at the pleasure of the president or legislators and supposedly can be removed with ease. All the rest are civil servants. For practical purposes they can be removed only by death, resignation, or the grossest sort of malfeasance in office.

The situation in state and local governments is not much improved. State legislators, city councilmen, mayors, governors, a few state officials, some judges, school board members and the like are elected. The rest — an estimated eight or nine million employees — are either appointed or untouchable.

Elections seldom offer a serious choice of alternatives. There have been elections in the past when voters were offered a definite choice of programs by presidential candidates and their parties. Perhaps the last one where the choice was major was 1932, when Franklin D. Roosevelt badly beat Herbert Hoover. Most elections, be it for president, governor, mayor, or most legislative seats, present a choice, as the expression goes, between Tweedle-dee and Tweedle-dum. When all the campaign oratory is over, the voters have made a choice based on the personality of the candidate, his appearance, his oratory, his past performances in office, if any — or maybe just their negative feelings about all these things concerning his opponent. At best Americans register a protest concerning their prevailing dissatisfaction with such things as war, unemployment, high prices, taxation, corruption. Voters have only the scantiest information about the views of candidates on these and other matters of public interest — if indeed the candidates have any views.

The American electorate troops to the polls by the tens of millions to vote one set of candidates into office and another set out. But what happens? Not very much. There are a few new programs, a different style, some strange faces, but the conduct of government — be it at City Hall, the State House, or in Washington — goes on much as it had before, and so do the problems. Nothing very startling happens. Nothing remotely revolutionary occurs.

Although their campaign oratory may have given a different impression, there were, in practice, no basic, essential differences between the political attitudes and philosophies of Richard Nixon and Hubert Humphrey in 1968; Lyndon Johnson and Barry Goldwater in 1964; Richard Nixon and John F. Kennedy in 1960; Dwight Eisenhower and Adlai Stevenson in 1956 and 1952; Harry Truman and Thomas Dewey in 1948. It is reasonable to conjecture that the course of American history would have changed very slightly, and the changes would have been peripheral and transient had the defeated candidates been the victors. The American political system guarantees that this will be so in all but most exceptional times.

The United States is a corporate state. The nation is run by a power structure composed of top politicians and military leaders supported, financed, and maintained by giant American corporations. The result is a government operating for the benefit of politicians, military leaders and, especially, corporations. Democracy, if not dead, is dying. The unresponsiveness of government and the frustration of people trying to control it are rooted in the unresponsiveness and the power needs of the ruling elite.

The corporate state operates for the benefit of itself, which means war, high profits, tax policies favorable to business, large government expenditures with corporations. All of this means that government policies and spending cannot be geared for peace, elimination of poverty, improvement of cities, pollution control, and other programs of benefit to the people.

Politics is a basically dishonest profession. Politicians are responsive largely to those who provide the most money in the form of campaign contributions and to those large pressure groups who can deliver votes, such as labor, ethnic, veteran and other organizations. Both the money and the votes and thus the politician are controlled by bosses. To the rest of the people, the politician offers a smokescreen of smiles, pious platitudes, glittering generalities, and downright deceit.

A credibility gap exists between the words of many, perhaps most, politicians and their performances. The federal government in particular often operates behind a screen of official secrecy, concealing its actions and mishaps behind a "top secret" stamp. This not only hides information from the people but enables government officials to do just about anything they want and later offer whatever explanation they believe will be most palatable.

A significant number of politicians are "on the take." If they are not helping themselves to tax funds, they are operating for the benefit of large campaign contributors.

The Bill of Rights is more myth than fact. The freedoms of speech, press, and assembly guaranteed in the Constitution exist only for the rich, wellborn, and white. As the jails and prisons attest, the poor and the black do not get equal justice from the police and the courts. There is a determined effort by the police to stamp out dissent, particularly when it takes the form of long hair, unusual clothing, unindustrious habits, black skin, and unpopular political or economic opinions. Such dissenters are being raided, arrested on trumped-up charges, physically brutalized on a more or less regular basis. The courts give one form of justice to a man who can afford a lawyer, quite a different one to the person who can't. He may languish in jail for weeks or months just to come to a trial in which he is declared innocent or convicted of a minor misdemeanor calling for a fine or a few days in jail. Only some are free in this land.

The above, I believe, is a brief but fair summation of the major criticisms of the American political system. The summation was deliberately done without rhetoric or lapses into personalities. I chose this method, not as a put-down of these criticisms, but to honor them. They are legitimate criticisms believed by a large number of intelligent and informed people. They are also most serious. They deserve to be and need to be treated seriously. And they have been. Long before the protests and the rhetoric started, political scientists were writing about these problems, analyzing their causes and proffering solutions.

This book is going to be largely about these criticisms. All will be elaborated in more detail, and others will be cited. This process should begin with the statement that there is another side to this coin of criticisms.

Unresponsive? Congress passed and the states duly ratified with amazing rapidity the twenty-sixth amendment to the Constitution giving the vote to eighteen-, nineteen-, and twenty-year-olds. This government action occurred after state legislatures had refused previously to enfranchise younger voters, and after voters in several states had voted down such amendments to state constitutions.

Why was the amendment passed? It is possible to be politically cynical about it. Congress was Democratic and contained several members trying desperately to unseat Mr. Nixon, a Republican, from the White House. The Democrats believed that a large portion of the younger vote would go to their party and so favored it. The Democratic leadership then acted with great political skill. The eighteen-year-old vote was passed as a simple law requiring a simple majority in Congress. The legality of this was challenged and it went to the Supreme Court, which ruled that the law was valid in federal elections but not in state elections. That meant that teenagers could vote for president, vice president, senators, and congressmen, but for no one else. The states would have to maintain separate voter registration books and print separate ballots for young people. To avoid this confusion and expense, Congress re-enacted the eighteen-year-old vote as an amendment to the Constitution, easily amassing the needed two-thirds majority. It went to the states and was quickly ratified to avoid the imposssible mess that failure to ratify would have brought.

Perhaps the motive of the Democratic party was political, but there may have been another motive. At least the effect is the same. Much of the dissent, demonstrations, violence, and agitation of recent years has occurred among the young. It is the young more than any who feel the government is unresponsive. Giving young people the vote and involving them in the political process is certainly one way to end the criticisms they are voicing about the political process.

No control by the people? A corporate state? At the urging of consumer groups, Congress passed laws requiring auto makers to install safety devices on cars and ordered manufacturers to develop improved emission-control devices to ease the nation's air pollution problems. A contract for a supersonic airliner was canceled. Local residents have successfully fought factories and power plants and shopping centers which they believed would spoil the environment. Many examples could be cited to show that the people have successfully obtained beneficial legislation and fought corporate power when they went about it the right way.

Civil liberties dead? Wounded perhaps, but not deceased. Along with such things as the killings at Kent, Ohio, and Jackson, Mississippi, the shooting of prisoners at Attica, New York, the brutal excess of police, the use of troops to repress dissent, the political trials on dubious charges, the many instances when minorities did not have equality under the law and when due process of the law was more process than due must go the instances in which hundreds of thousands of people gathered peacefully advocating civil rights or peace; the exoneration of many of the Black Panthers at their trials; abolition of Jim Crow segregation in public places; extension of the vote to youth and black; greater protection for defendants at trials; the defense of newspapers' right to publish the Pentagon Papers which exposed America's somewhat unsavory entry into the Vietnam War. In truth, an excellent case could be made for the statement that Americans enjoy more civil liberties today than ever in history. That is perhaps a very small boast, for our liberty has always been more myth than fact.

These examples are cited not out of any artificial effort to achieve a balanced viewpoint, nor to prove the criticisms wrong. They are cited because they are simple facts to be strung out alongside the facts that are critical.

The point is that America is a big country and cut up into a tremendous mass of election districts. There are — believe it — 87,371 separate governmental units in the United States, including cities, counties, townships, school districts, water districts, and so on. The System is surely complicated. Because it is, no flat statement can be made about it that is wholly true. What may seem to be happening in Washington, D.C. is not what is actually happening in Tuscaloosa, Portland, Kensett, Arkansas — or the whole state of Arkansas. Ours is a big, varied country and the political system embraces it all.

But, of course, when a person indicts The System he is talking about the federal government, mostly. And so will we, mostly.

2

A Divided Nation

ANY UNDERSTANDING OF The System, its faults and virtues, must begin with the land and those who populate it. There must be an awareness of history, the converging forces that wrought change, the simple human efforts to control or at least survive the elements, the plagues, earning a living, finding a place to live, fulfilling the basic needs for food, clothing, shelter, and protection — in a word, life.

An awareness of our past will reveal, for example, that most of the serious and disturbing problems in the United States today are of recent origin, going back about twenty-five years or less.

Only recently has the United States had widespread affluence. For most of our history the problem was widespread poverty. There were the rich, to be sure, and periods in which the middle and lower classes had extra money. But the boom or bust cycle that dominated America's economy until 1940 made it impossible for the great majority of the population to accumulate wealth or its appurtenances. Only in the last quarter century have the bulk of Americans purchased a house, car, furniture, appliances, fur coats and other luxuries, traveled widely, sent their children to college, and felt the drive for and ability to get still more. We are simply not very used to coping with the problems of affluence.

Only since 1945 or even 1950 has the United States had a large standing military force. Always before America was largely disarmed, beefing up its military force only in times of war. We just have not had much experience in coping with the economic, social, and political effects of a large military force. History is not much help in solving these problems.

The United States was not very much involved in world affairs until 1945. There was a brief flurry of international activity in 1919 when President Woodrow Wilson participated in the European peace talks following World War I. But the nation quickly retired from the scene and refused to participate in most world organizations aimed at preserving peace. Our history is almost entirely isolationist. We hid behind our ocean frontiers, tended to our own affairs, and refused to involve ourselves in European and Asian problems. There were exceptions involving excursions into imperialism in the Caribbean, Latin America, and the Philippines. But only since World War II has the United States become an international interventionist on a major scale. Problems have inevitably resulted from this new role.

Television has been in large-scale use in America for only a quarter of a century. It has had tremendous impact on almost everything, for it permits people to sit in their living rooms and see and hear nearly anything happening in the world. The war in Vietnam is not being fought alone in some far-off corner of the world, but in the homes of millions of Americans. We see men walk and ride on the moon, riots across the nation or the world, governments overthrown, politicians acting foolishly, new products being offered for sale and much, much more. Seeing and hearing an event at the time it is happening has a tremendous emotional and intellectual impact. Much of what is happening in America and its political system is an effort to understand this new medium and to control it and the problems it creates.

America has had a race problem since 1619, when the first slaves were brought ashore, if not before. We have engaged in near ceaseless strife ever since, including a Civil War, countless hangings, beatings, and bloodletting, all in the name of race. But only fifteen years ago did the American Negro begin to achieve substantial and effective civil equality. Only in 1955 did he begin to learn to use for his own benefit the political tools that white Americans use. Neither the black man nor the white has had much practice at these new exercises.

Many other serious problems are of recent origin, including: scientific understanding of basic life processes; prolongation of life; elimination of many diseases that scourged man until recently; technology leading to automation and reduced need for unskilled and semi-skilled labor; the widespread and chronic poverty that results; overpopulation; the simple aging of cities, homes, factories so they must be replaced; a high level of mobility in which 20 percent of the population is moving its place of residence at any given moment. All this is new in America. I'm sure the reader could add to the list.

There is perhaps an inevitable human tendency to solve new problems by applying methods that worked in the past. We regulate commercial airlines — and mass airline travel is a new phenomenon — by essentially the same methods railroads were regulated nearly a century ago. We license and regulate television by essentially the same method as we did radio, even though the media are radically different. When a congressional committee asked to see the unedited film taken for a controversial CBS television program on the Department of Defense in 1971, the network shielded itself behind a banner labeled "freedom of the press" and few suggested that the press and television are two radically different things.

Faced with high unemployment and rising prices — a most unusual combination — we turn to the methods of the 1930s and 1940s, at best, or more likely we cling to the tenets of *laissez faire* capitalism of a century ago. Fearing the menace of Communism, be it of the Soviet or Chinese variety, we select the methods of the past, a system of alliances and intervention by armed force. Encountering militant dissent from black people, peace protestors, and other large groups of the dissatisfied, there is a tendency to reply with repression, using police and troops, mass arrests, and political trials.

It is axiomatic that new problems call for new solutions. Why is America having such great difficulty agreeing on what the problems are, let alone how to solve them? This inability to define problems, to agree upon and work out sensible solutions quickly is what the shouting and protests and criticism of The System are all about.

Why are we so slow in solving our problems? Why do we let them go so long that they become extremely difficult to solve? Why can we not agree on what to do and then go about doing it?

Answers to these most important questions must begin with an examination of the forces that shaped America. We are a most diverse lot inhabiting a huge land. In the beginning we were populated by Indians, Pilgrims, Puritans, Catholics, Jews, Spanish, Dutch, Swedes, Germans, blacks, half-blacks, and a few others. We were rich, poor, ambitious, indolent, thrifty, intelligent and ignorant, clever and imitative.

To this already considerable mixture was added, through immigration, an incredible array of peoples until we became the melting pot of nations. Between 1850 and 1930, the United States accepted over thirty-five million direct immigrants to its shores. And that figure does not count several millions of Europeans and Africans who came or were brought into the country prior to 1850. We became a nation of all races — Indians, whites, blacks, Chinese, and mixtures of all those races. All religions, including those of the Orient, were included. A vast array of languages was spoken even into the third and fourth generations. Even today there are large numbers of Americans who can speak English but feel more comfortable in Chinese, Italian, Polish, or other tongues.

For a long time the simple size of the land absorbed all these people. The unhappy, dissatisfied, unlucky, or ambitious could always go off somewhere and find a piece of virgin ground on which he could determine his own destiny. He could clear it and till it, grow crops and raise animals and perhaps become rich. But if not so lucky or able, at least he was independent and reasonably self-sufficient, master of his own fate. This possibility continued well into this century. But it is long gone today in the continental United States. Only Alaska still offers it, and it is rapidly disappearing there.

If there is such a thing as the national character, this desire to be alone on one's land is a key part of it. Robert Ardrey would speak of "the territorial imperative."[1] Today we see it in the flight to the suburbs, the massive outpouring of people to the greenswards where they buy a small piece of land with a house on it, grow flowers, fight crab grass, then get into their car — itself another little island of territory — and fight their way through horrendous traffic back downtown to their jobs. We see it in the young people joining communes, the number of people who have quit or dream about quitting the "rat race" and buying a farm someplace, the large numbers who have moved abroad. Only recently, in Tulsa, Oklahoma, a group of people were discovered holding parties in the city's storm drains, for there they could be alone and undisturbed to do their thing.

This desire to go off alone or in small groups is perhaps integral in the American nature, derived somehow from the land we inhabit and our experiences with it. Other nations do not have the small family farm. In many others parts of the world, farmers live in villages from which they venture forth to till the fields — often owned by others. Some nationalities are content with a rented home in a village or an apartment. Americans have a thirst for land. We are homeless without it.

Our territorial nature has led to division — the Texan, the Californian, the Southerner, the New Yorker, the Midwesterner, and many more. We are divided by land, by customs, by dialects even of English let alone foreign languages, by attitudes and ways of life.

Atop this come other divisions: the rich and the poor, the landed and the unlanded, the educated and the ignorant. We are divided by religion. Consider the divisions among labor and business. The latter is divided into the capitalist, the manager of the corporation, and the small businessman. Labor has always been bereft of unity. There are skilled workers organized into craft unions such as pipefitters and bricklayers; then the industrial workers organized on an industry-wide basis, such as steel and auto workers. There are further divisions among blue-collar industrial workers, white-collar business workers, service workers, and government employees. The history of the United States has been much influenced by the failure of American workers to unite, as they united in Britain with the formation of the Labour party.

The intellectuals separate themselves into specialties. There are anatomists and zoologists, engineers, physicians and physicists, chemists, geologists, psychiatrists, and psychologists, and experts in nearly everything. All have developed a special terminology which frequently bears little resemblance to English. Each has its rituals, excesses, and articles of faith. America's intellectual community couldn't possibly be more divided.

The divisions among us are immense. It is not possible to name them all, but some are: farmers and non-farmers, veterans and non-veterans; joiners of lodges and such organizations and those who do not believe in such things; those who believe in a strong military posture and its use and those who abhor it; intellectuals who believe in the mind and its uses and those who distrust it; those who want a beautiful, unpolluted America and those who would surrender it for jobs and money; those who wish to encourage arts and leisure and those who want science and work; those who believe in full equality for women and those who think they belong in the home and maternity ward; those who believe in the virtues of work and independence; and those who think a greater application of government will achieve the good life. The list is endless.

Today as through history we have been able as a people to agree on certain essentials — the value of personal liberty, defense of the nation, protection of basic institutions, such as, to use the popular parlance, God, flag, and Mom. And there are many who will disagree with all those.

On everything else we divide. We disagree, argue, quarrel. We form special interest groups to belabor a certain viewpoint on almost any issue. We have labor, business, veterans, women's peace, war, farm, conservative, liberal, and hosts of other groups. We lobby in the governments. We try to force our will. The result of the disagreement is delay and more delay. We are a divided nation. It is The System.

We may find some comfort in the fact that other large, diverse nations have done little better. Russia and China, after centuries of despotic monarchy, in modern times each found some form of unity only under a totalitarian dictatorship. India, after almost two hundred years of colonial rule under Britain, won independence and immediately divided into India and Pakistan on the basis of religion. They have more or less been at each other's throats ever since. Even small, relatively homogeneous countries have had difficulties. Spain, which does not have nearly the divisions of America, has been united only under a dictatorship or a monarchy. Italy has never been able to find a stable government other than a dictatorship. Germany is today divided. At this writing even so small a people as the Irish are killing each other by the score over a single issue, religion. Only such small, homogeneous nations as Britain, the Scandinavian countries, and the Low Countries of Belgium and Holland have been able to create a relatively stable republican government. Perhaps the American process has something to recommend it.

We must here, however, confront a simple fact. The divisions among us, our failure to identify problems and agree upon solutions, have long been exacerbated by our system of government. We glorify disunity and make unity grossly difficult. It is this we must take up next.

3

A Design for Deadlock and Drift

SOME YEARS AGO, a small group of university political scientists seriously suggested that a new convention be impaneled to rewrite the United States Constitution. Their suggestion was duly reported in the press largely because of its novelty. Such a proposal smacked of flag-pole sitting or a competition to see who could fly the farthest by flapping his arms while jumping off a high building. It was silly.

These political scientists undoubtedly knew and took comfort in the fact that no less than Thomas Jefferson had proposed that the Constitution be revised every so often, on the order of once every generation.

Let us [not] weakly believe that one generation is not as capable as another of taking care of itself, and of ordering its own affairs. Let us . . . avail ourselves of our reason and experience to correct the crude essays of our first and unexperienced, although wise, virtuous and well-meaning counsels. And, lastly, let us provide in our Constitution for its revision at stated periods. What these periods should be, nature herself indicates. . . . Each generation is as independent of the one preceding, as that was of all which had gone before. It has, then, like them, a right to choose for itself the form of government it believes most promotive of its own happiness . . . and it is for the peace and good of mankind that a solemn opportunity of doing this every nineteen or twenty years should be provided by the Constitution.[1]

Jefferson said and wrote many wise words, for more than any other of the Founding Fathers he believed in the wisdom of the people and their ability to govern themselves. He believed in majority rule and in democracy. Yet his proposal for a regular revision of the Constitution, as well as his statement that a little rebellion from time to time fertilizes the tree of liberty, are generally considered by most people as not among the great man's most inspired utterances. He must have said both things tongue in cheek.

There is no suggestion here that the Constitution be rewritten. That noble artifact has been "sanctified" in America, as Professor Henry Steele Commager put it.[2] Our basic law, the blueprint for our government, it is honored above all else in our heritage, including the Declaration of Independence. To alter it in any significant way is unthinkable. There is also the practical difficulty of selecting people as wise as the original drafters were, as well as incorporating into a new document all the laws, court decisions, and practices which have already altered the Constitution through almost two hundred years.

The System is rooted in the Constitution. Time has brought many changes in the practice of government in America. These will be taken up later. What is important to realize now is that many of the difficulties which lead people to denounce The System are built into the Constitution, as well as why they were.

The Constitution was written during a hot, muggy summer of 1787 in Philadelphia. At that time the nation consisted of thirteen states strung along the Eastern seaboard. The first census of 1790 counted less than four million citizens, including those hardy souls who had moved to Maine, Vermont, and across the Appalachians into Kentucky and Tennessee. The fastest means of communication and transportation were the sailboat on water and the horse on land. The nation was overwhelmingly agricultural: small farms in the North and West; large plantations in the South where tobacco, indigo, and sugar cane were grown with slave labor. Cotton would not become king for a few years, because Eli Whitney had not yet invented his gin to make its cultivation profitable. Such industries as existed were small, generally of the handicraft variety. The nation was almost wholly dependent upon Europe for its manufactured products.

The delegates who drafted the Constitution that summer were a distinguished lot. All things considered, they were about the best the young nation could produce at the time. A few of the great were missing. Thomas Jefferson was in Paris as America's ambassador. John

Adams was ambassador to London. But both managed to influence the deliberations through correspondence. Patrick Henry and Sam Adams, the old firebrands of the Revolution, were absent and not sorely missed. Henry was named a delegate, but refused because he was suspicious.

But those who remained were amply equal to the task: George Washington, Benjamin Franklin, James Madison, Alexander Hamilton, Roger Sherman, Oliver Ellsworth, Gouverneur Morris, John Dickinson, the two Charles Pinckneys, George Mason—fifty-five in all. The drafters were men of property, education, and influence. They were men of moderate and conservative views. The "common man" they hardly were.

And they were young. One Charles Pinckney was 29, the other 41; Alexander Hamilton, 30; Rufus King, 32; Jonathan Dayton of New Jersey, 26; Gouverneur Morris, 35; James Madison, 36. Even when Benjamin Franklin's 81 years were included, the average age of the delegates was only 43.

They were also experienced in government. Nearly three fourths had sat in the Continental Congress. Many had helped to write their state constitutions. Eight had signed the Declaration of Independence, seven had been state governors, and twenty-one had fought in the Revolutionary War. From Paris, Jefferson read the names of the delegates and called it "an assembly of demi-gods."

All of this is lore and legend, magnified and romanticized in apparently endless history and civics textbooks, biographies, novels, and plays. There is no virtue in adding to it here. It takes nothing away from the brilliance of these Founding Fathers — and they were brilliant — to take a hard look at what they did and the problems that have resulted.

We know precious little about what happened at the Convention. The delegates voted to keep their deliberations secret so all could speak freely. There would be no demagoguery, as little pressure from outside as possible. Parallels today would be an executive session of a congressional committee, an international confab, or a collective bargaining session between labor and management. No record of the proceeding exists other than Madison's "Notes." A great deal of material was written after the convention as part of the ratification campaign, most notably *The Federalist*, penned by Madison and Hamilton. But it would defy human nature to suppose that these after-the-fact writings did not include at least some hindsight and self-serving.

These prominent, able, and young men disagreed heatedly and argued vigorously. It is reasonable to assume that the Convention would have disbanded entirely had not the delegates met in an atmosphere of crisis. The nation, endeavoring to govern itself under the Articles of Confederation, was coming apart at the seams. There was no strong national leadership. Individual states were bickering, putting up barriers to trade, seeming on the verge of open war over ownership of western lands. The people were poor and suffering from the after-effects of the war. The currency was so bad it was hardly worth the description. Open rebellion had broken out in Massachusetts, and was put down only with difficulty. Something simply had to be done or these thirteen states, all with common language and common origins, would go thirteen different ways, leaving the nation no nation at all. The British fully expected this to happen.

The delegates had to cope with an array of attitudes that were often conflicting. The American people, the delegates included, were devotees of John Locke's philosophy of human rights. The Declaration of Independence had said it: every man has an "inalienable" right to life, liberty, and the pursuit of happiness. Individual freedom was not some hoary textbook principle in those days. It was a live, breathing reality to most of the people. Infringement of it was an invitation to grab a gun.

At the same time the people were loyal to the law. They believed in the law (if not a lot of it) duly passed by representatives of the people elected to form legislatures for this purpose. They believed in at least a certain amount of compliance with the law as long as it did not curtail individual freedom too much.

Many of the people and nearly all the delegates had, however, an instant distrust of democracy. It was inconceivable that the mass of the poor, hungry, dirty, poorly educated could govern. The mass of people were viewed as filled with instant passions easily inflamed by demagogues and self-serving destroyers of liberty. Curtailment of these passionate excesses was essential.

There was nearly universal distrust of strong executive powers. Many states had constitutions calling for only the most impotent of governors. The Revolution had been fought to get out from under British Royal Governors. It seemed nonsensical to reinstate them after freedom was won. It was a nearly automatic assumption that a strong executive would inevitably become a king or a tyrant.

Finally, the people had no highly developed conception of themselves as Americans. The term was used, but they gave at least equal importance (and probably more) to being a Virginian or Pennsylvanian or New Yorker.

The brilliance of the Founding Fathers is that they found, through argument and compromise, *some* way to resolve these conflicting ideas to form a government that offered at least a promise of being effective.

They concocted a federal system, which hardly existed anywhere in the world. The nation was too big, its problems too varied, the roles of the states too important ever to have a unitary system work. (An example of where it does work is the English system wherein most of the government occurs in London.)

To make the federal system work — and some historians consider this the single most brilliant achievement of the Convention — the Founding Fathers devised what amounts to a dual system of government. A person is a citizen of both the state in which he resides and of the United States. Patrick Henry, who had worried a lot about it, could thus be both a Virginian and an American.

Certain essential powers were taken from the states and given to the federal government, such as military defense, foreign affairs, regulation of interstate commerce, coinage, a post office, patents, and the like. Federal powers were clearly spelled out and thus limited. The states were left sovereignty over everything else. When the Bill of Rights was added as the first ten amendments to the Constitution at the time of ratification, it was further specified that all powers not residing with the federal government or the states belonged to the people.

This federal system is still with us today, although greatly altered.

The delegates rejected democracy. The American people do not govern themselves, never have, and chances are never will. There is a practical problem with a democracy—usually called a pure democracy. It can operate only in a small place where all or most of the citizens can get together to pass laws and decide matters of policy. It exists today in only a few small towns of New England and in some Swiss cantons. It was simply impractical to conceive of four million Americans deciding anything.

Nor were the delegates very impressed with democracy as a means of government. Ancient Greece hadn't fared very well under it. Government should be by the best and ablest and most informed people acting for the people or in the name of the people so as to care for their welfare and best interests. This philosophy was expressed later by Abraham Lincoln. "The function of the government is to do for the people that which they cannot, nor will not do for themselves." It is of more than passing interest that such a philosophy of government was also heartily embraced by Lenin.

But the Founding Fathers also abhorred anything remotely resembling monarchy, tyranny, or despotism. To avoid the pitfalls of both democracy and tyranny, the delegates voted for a *republic*. In this, the governors are neither democratic nor tyrannical. They are, it is hoped, the best and wisest of men (like the delegates!), elected by the people to govern them in the best and wisest manner. A republic offers the advantage of securing the public good and private rights against either the popular passions of majorities or of despotism, while preserving "the spirit and form of popular government," as Madison expressed it in the tenth Federalist paper.

Nothing is more cunning in the Constitution (or important to The System today) than the efforts of the Founding Fathers to steer that republic through the twin shoals of democracy and tyranny.

"Since angels do not govern men," as Madison put it in *The Federalist*, No. 47, "ways must be found for men to govern themselves." With the angels out of it, it seemed to Madison and men of his persuasion that one of only three things could happen in government. First, a person or a group of persons could impose a tyranny on the people; second, a majority faction of the people in a democracry or a republic could impose its rule on a minority with a result of tyranny again; or, third, a minority, by using disruptive tactics, could throttle all efforts of the majority to govern, resulting in anarchy (which is government by angels) or still another form of tyranny. Much of what the Constitution is about is an effort to find a fourth way to a government that avoids the pitfalls of the above three.

As originally written, not as later amended, the Constitution made it extremely difficult for either tyranny or democracy to thrive. Tyranny was avoided by granting most of the powers of the federal government to Congress, which was democraticized by having one of its houses, the larger, elected directly by the people. As a further safeguard against tyranny, the members of the House of Representatives were elected for only a two-year term, giving the people a quick chance, if they wished, to thwart any despotic plans. Certain key functions, such as electing the president in event of a deadlock, were granted to the House. Also, all tax legislation had to initiate in the House. The power to tax is the power to destroy. The people should be safeguarded against this.

The delegates worried about nothing so much as the presidency, for there was where tyranny would occur, if anywhere. Delegates argued and argued and argued over the office. Fearing despotism, many delegates wanted none at all or only a most weak and ceremonial chief executive. But the experience under the Articles of Confederation, indeed throughout the Revolution itself, showed clearly the need for an individual to administer the laws, command the armed forces, conduct foreign policy, appoint ambassadors and other public officials, and provide dynamic leadership. Very late in the Convention, as if they were simply worn out from all the argument, the Founding Fathers voted for such a man — the man who sat in front of them, George Washington. Everyone knew he would be the first president. The office was designed for him. As Benjamin Franklin told the Convention, "The first man at the helm will be a good one. Nobody knows what sort may come afterwards."[3]

Further efforts to prevent presidential tyranny were

made. His term was limited to four years* and he was required to be a native-born citizen of at least age 35. In those days a man of that age was considered mature, settled, and possibly past his prime. The president had no power to tax or to make laws. Other restrictions were placed on the powers he was granted. If all else failed a truly bad president could be impeached and removed from office.

How was he to be elected? Perhaps no greater puzzle faced the delegates. The solution was one of their least inspired. He could not be hereditary, for that was monarchy. There really was no suitable person or organization to appoint him. He had to be elected. By whom? Direct election by the people was out. That was an invitation to tyranny: the despot, the "man on the white horse," the demagogue whipping up the passions of the people to install him in office, keeping him there till tyranny was established.

Could Congress elect the president? Many delegates thought so. It was a key point in the original plan for government offered by Virginia. But a persuasive group of the delegates successfully argued that the president had to be independent of the legislative branch. Otherwise he would be its slave, limited in his leadership, creating the sort of chaos with which many states were afflicted at the time.

The Convention finally adopted a fuzzy plan called the Electoral College to elect the president. Each state

---

*Nothing specific was said, however, to prevent his being reelected for any number of terms. The limit of two terms came years later, as the twenty-second amendment.

was to appoint—it was never said how or by whom the appointments were to be made—electors equal to the total number of senators and representatives which the state had in Congress. These electors were to meet in their *respective* states—there was no provision for their assembling for deliberations—and vote for two men as president. The man receiving the most votes was to be president, the man receiving the second highest number of votes was to be vice president.

In the event no one individual received a majority of the electoral votes, the election was to occur in the House of Representatives, on the basis of one vote per state. The delegates, wise and far-seeing in so many things, surely knew this system was filled with pitfalls. It would undoubtedly suffice to elect George Washington, which is about all it did. They apparently believed that, thereafter, the elections for practical purposes would be decided in the House of Representatives, for the electors would hardly be able to agree on anyone.*

The convention also worked assiduously to eliminate the possible dangers of democracy. The House of Representatives was to be popularly elected as a counterweight to the president. But it must be remembered that in those days the vote was severly restricted. Property qualifications alone kept most of the "rabble" out of the polling places.

If the House sought to vent its passions to the detriment of the nation, great obstacles were placed in its way. The president was formidable. Even more formida-

---

*Though the Electoral College still exists, of course, the electors have, for many years, simply followed the majority vote of the people in each state.

ble was the Senate. This was to be based, not on population, but on equal representation among the states. Each state had two senators, permitting the small states equal power with the large ones. This alone would counteract the effect of population.

Then, the senators were given six-year terms, with one-third of the members to be elected every two years. The longer terms were intended to make the Senate a more deliberative body, less likely to be inflamed by the passions of the moment because its members were more secure in their positions.

Most importantly, the senators were indirectly, not directly, elected by the people. They were chosen by the state legislatures, which were, of course, elected by the people. Being one extra step away from the people would surely be a precaution against too much democracy. The Senate was given exclusive powers to "advise and consent" with the president over appointments, treaties, and the like. The House might bring charges of impeachment against the president, but the more deliberative Senate would try him.

Finally, as an additional safeguard against both tyranny and democracy, an independent court system was set up. The Supreme Court was to consist of judges named by the president but approved by the Senate. Thereafter, it was to be left alone to decide cases according to the laws of the land.

Madison is called the "father of the Constitution" and perhaps not too exaggeratedly so. In *The Federalist* he spoke of his fear of tyranny either by a majority running roughshod over the minority or the latter imposing its will on the majority. How were such forms of tyranny to be prevented?

The first step, under the Constitution, was separation of powers among the executive, legislative, and judicial branches. Each was independent of the other. But what if a president, Congress, and Supreme Court justices got together? Wouldn't that lead to tyranny of either a majority or minority as the case might be?

This was to be prevented by the second step, a system of checks and balances. A clever morass of these were developed. To name a few: the president was dependent upon Congress for taxes and appropriations, his appointments had to be confirmed, his treaties ratified; Congress was to be checked by the different construction and constituencies of the two branches and the president was given a veto over congressional laws, a veto made especially difficult to overturn; the judiciary was appointed by the president and approved by the Senate, and its entire structure could be altered by a simple act of Congress. No branch of government, Madison hoped, would be able to act entirely on its own. Each would be dependent on the other branches, even though separate and independent.

The third step was a cunning inclusion of human nature into the Constitution. Madison wrote in the tenth Federalist paper:

> The great security against a gradual concentration of the several powers in the same department, consists in giving to those who administer each department the necessary constitutional means and *personal motives* to resist encroachments of the others. (Emphasis added.)

Again Madison wrote in the fifty-first paper:

> Ambition must be made to counteract ambition. The
> interest of the man must be connected with the constitu-
> tional rights of the place.

In his book *The Deadlock of Democracy*, political
scientist James MacGregor Burns addressed himself to
Madison's phrase:

> "Ambition must be made to counteract ambition" — in
> these seven words Madison drove straight to the heart
> of the whole problem; here he showed his genius as a
> political scientist. For he was not content with a flimsy
> separation of power that lunging politicians could smash
> through like paper. He was calling for barricade after
> barricade against the thrust of a popular majority — and
> the ultimate and impassable barricade was a system of
> checks and balances that would use man's essential
> human nature — his interests, his passions, his ambi-
> tions — to control itself. For Madison's ultimate checks
> and balances were political; they built into the engine of
> government automatic stabilizing devices that were sure
> to counterbalance one another because they were pow-
> ered by separate sources of political energy. The ambi-
> tions of Presidents and Senators and Representatives
> and judges were bound to collide because each was re-
> sponsible to separate constituencies in the "greater vari-
> ety of parties and interests of the new Federal republic."
> And each official, of course, had some kind of constitu-
> tional weapon — the President's veto, for example, or the
> Senators' power over treaties — that could be used
> against other officials and the sectional or economic or
> ideological interests they represented.[4]

All this to prevent majority rule. And more. So fear-
ful were the founders of a majority dominating a minori-

ty that they larded the document, particularly when the Bill of Rights was added, with every conceivable safeguard of individual liberty and minority rights. Speech, press, religion, assembly, the bearing of arms, trial by jury, the writ of habeas corpus are all guaranteed. No man may lose his freedom or property without due process of law. No man may be forced to testify against himself. A person accused of treason must be confronted by two witnesses. No Bill of Attainder or ex post facto law may be enacted. The list goes on and on. Minority rights are built into the Constitution in layers. The document absolutely insures there will be dissent in America.

Why all this protection of minorities? Why make it so difficult for the majority to rule because of separation of powers, checks and balances, and the playing off of ambition against ambition? And the Founding Fathers did exactly that. Many have decried this, including historian Henry Steele Commager in his book *Majority Rule and Minority Rights:*

> . . . the framers of our Constitution confused, it would seem, jurisdiction with power, and the confusion has persisted down to our own day. They failed properly to distinguish between the authority government should have and the manner in which government might exercise that authority which it did have. They set up limits on the jurisdiction of government, enumerating things no government could do; and this was eminently proper and in harmony with the philosophy of the Revolutionary era. But they went further. So fearful were they of governmental tyranny that even where they granted to government certain necessary powers they put obstacles

in the way of the effective exercise of those powers. They set up not only boundaries to government but impediments in government. Thus, they not only make it difficult for government to invade fields denied to it, but they make it difficult for government to operate at all. They created a system where deadlock would be the normal character of the American government. . . .[5]

Why all the efforts by the founders to hamstring government action? Why all these extraordinary measures to protect the minority, make it difficult to form a majority opinion in the government to enact laws, administer programs, and benefit the public good?

Professor Burns points out that there was no great divisiveness in the country to necessitate such extraordinary steps. The people were reasonably devoted to liberty and the natural rights of man. He believes the "key to Madison's thinking" was "to stop people from turning easily to government for help." He adds: "Government, in short, was a necessary evil that must be curbed, not an instrument for the realization of man's higher ideals or a nation's broader interests."[6]

The result of the built-in barricades to thwart the rule of a "tyrannical" majority has ever since been delay, delay, more delay, followed by inaction. Burns calls it the "old cycle of deadlock and drift." His exposition of it is excellent:

Historically there has been a serious lag—once a near fatal lag—in the speed and effectiveness with which the national government has coped with emerging crises.

The record is a disturbing one. The steady, moderate action on slavery that was so desperately needed in the 1840s and 1850s finally came, immoderately and at a frightful cost, in the 1860s and 1870s. American participation in the first real efforts at collective security came after World War II instead of World War I. The anti-depression measures so critically necessary in the 1930s, if not long before, became governmental and political commitments only in the 1940s and 1950s. The most elementary types of federal control over economic power were delayed for years. The social security and other welfare measures needed to protect men from the insecurities of the modern economy should have been adopted at least by the turn of the century; they had to wait for the New Deal in the 1930s. The economic internationalism that characterized the Marshall Plan and its successor programs in the last fifteen years was missing in the 1920s, when our nationalistic economic policies helped bring on the world depression. Our admirable concern today with the developing countries would have paid off many times over if we had come to it sooner; as it is, we are trying to influence revolutions that in many cases have moved out of the narrow orbit of American influence. The cost of delay has also been high in countless other areas of hardly less importance: urban decline, conservation, tax reform, medical care, governmental organizations. We have reacted to change rather than dominated it.

We have often been too late, and we have been too late with too little. (Emphasis added.)[7]

It is difficult to think of a single reform in American history which did not take decades to accomplish. Often such reforms were delayed long after there was a clearly demonstrable majority favoring them. Consider only civil service reform; extension of the vote to the property-less, female, black, and youthful; civil rights for Negroes; child labor laws; wage and hour laws; safety acts; conservation. The list could go on to great length.

The United States has reached a point in its history

where it simply does not have much chance to luxuriate in decades of delay. Pollution, overpopulation, an arms race with nuclear weapons and intercontinental rockets, racial strife, urban decay, economic maldistribution of wealth, and other such problems have been building up over decades. They are explosive problems. They require a great deal of governmental action. The individual cannot solve them himself as in the days of Madison. The nation needs to find a way to form a majority and to take quick, effective action.

But it is simplistic to conclude that the Constitution is at fault in The System and must be discarded. It is true that the Constitution may have been written to make majority rule and any action by government difficult, but the problem has been aggravated over the years by many factors, including some of the efforts intended to make government more responsive.

In defense of the Constitution it must be remembered that the federal government has shown a number of times in crises and emergencies that it can take bold, quick action. It happened in most of our wars, in the New Deal in the 1930s, and for brief, if all too seldom, periods following the election of a strong and popular president. The most recent followed the election of Lyndon Johnson in 1964, when much progressive legislation was passed, such as Medicare, aid to education, voting rights for Negroes. Clearly some sort of mechanism exists under the present form of government which permits greater responsiveness to public needs. The problem must be to get it to run more smoothly and consistently. A search for this elusive mechanism surely can only be of value.

We can begin the search by saying that the Founding Fathers, after leaving the convention hall and facing the problem of running a government, quickly realized the basic problem with the Constitution; that is, simply finding enough unity to accomplish any sort of government. A solution to the deficiency was readily found. No less a personage than James Madison participated in founding the nation's first political party. From that action has come the best and the worst in America, our finest hopes for unity and progress and our bitterest disappointments. The System is intertwined with politics. We need to understand it.

4

Political Parties — A Need for Cement

THE CONSTITUTION MAKES no mention of political parties, and it is unlikely that the drafters were aware of them as they later developed in the United States. But they were aware of factions. Madison spoke of them at length in *The Federalist*, describing how he hoped the Constitution would prevent any faction from usurping power and controlling the government and the people.

The Constitution itself developed factions which led to political parties, however. Citizens aligned themselves into Federalists, who favored the Constitution, and Anti-Federalists who disliked it. The Federalist leadership consisted in the beginning mostly of the original drafters. The Anti-Federalists were led by such celebrated states righters as Patrick Henry.

With ratification of the Constitution, the Federalists

established the new government. A large portion of the first Senate consisted of men who had drafted the Constitution. The Federalists dominated throughout the terms of George Washington and John Adams, a total of twelve years. Thereafter the Federalists died, for they never were a political party in the true sense of the word. They were a collection of like-minded and brilliant men.

The origins of American political parties stem from the fiscal policies formulated by Alexander Hamilton and the clash between him and Thomas Jefferson over them. As Secretary of the Treasury, Hamilton was the financial genius of the first administration. Americans had little understanding of government finance, public debt, and banking. Perhaps that is why they distrusted bankers and tax collectors. Hamilton sought to put the nation on a sound financial footing and give validity to the nation's currency and credit.

His program, as adopted, called for a customs tariff with the duties on tonnage to favor American shipping. The foreign and domestic debt was funded at par; that is, the sum written on the bond. The Bank of the United States was chartered with authority to set up branches in other states. The program was highly successful. The stock of the Bank of the United States was subscribed within four hours. United States bonds were selling at above par in London and Amsterdam in 1791. Ample tax revenues enabled the United States to pay off the foreign debt in 1795 and the domestic debt in 1835, despite the expenses of the War of 1812.

Hamilton also wanted to encourage manufacturing by

imposing a protective tariff to keep out foreign goods, inducing skilled workers to immigrate, and encouraging inventions. But Congress took no action. Northern shipowners had too much at stake in shipping and trade to accept high tariffs that would discourage trade.

Hamilton's program seriously divided the nation, for its immediate benefits were not equally shared. The funding of the states' war debt at par was particularly controversial. The farmers, discharged veterans, and small shopkeepers who had taken government bonds in payment for services rendered, goods or money supplied during the war, had had to dispose of them at a fraction of their value in the hard times which followed the war. These securities were now in the hands of bankers, merchants, shippers, and other wealthy people. Being paid for these securities at par meant a huge windfall for the already rich.

Shipowners, traders, and those who financed them profited greatly from the discriminatory tonnage duties. In the major ports of New England and New York, these benefits trickled down through the population and led to good times. But not in Virginia. It had a population twice the size of Massachusetts or New York, yet in 1795 federal disbursements to citizens of that state in payment for debt were only $62,300. Massachusetts citizens received $309,500 and those of New York $367,000. Virginia planters had difficulty understanding why they were being taxed to pay off Yankees. Virginians had disposed of the federal bonds at a loss. Why shouldn't the Yankees?

Moreover, despite its generous coastline, Virginia had

little in the way of shipping and trading interests. An agricultural state, it depended upon New York and Massachusetts to ship its products to Europe. It felt most of the money was going to Northerners. Virginians felt anything but prosperous.

Virginians looked around for a person to lead them in protection of their interests and found him in Thomas Jefferson. Tall, sandy-haired, relaxed — we would call him "loose" or "cool" today — he was exactly what Virginia needed to counteract the ideas of Hamilton. In *The Oxford History of the American People*, historian Samuel Eliot Morison sought to portray the differences between these two giant men:

> Hamilton wished to concentrate power; Jefferson to diffuse power. Hamilton feared anarchy and thought in terms of order; Jefferson feared tyranny and thought in terms of liberty. Hamilton believed republican government could only succeed if directed by a governing elite; Jefferson that a republic must be based on an agrarian democracy. The people, according to Jefferson, were the safest and most virtuous, though not always the most wise, despository of power, and education would perfect their wisdom. Hamilton would diversify American economic life, encouraging shipping and creating manufactures by legislative enactment; Jefferson would have America remain a nation of farmers.[1]

It was the difference between New England and Virginia, North and South. One other cardinal difference must be mentioned. Hamilton, having never left the United States, was enamored of European political systems. Jefferson, having lived abroad, was enamored of America and its potential. Jefferson was never able to escape the notion that Hamilton, if left to his own devices, would establish a monarchy in America.

To counteract Hamilton and the Federalists and to gain the presidency for himself, Jefferson, aided by Madison, organized America's first political party. In defense of him (if he must have a defense) he did not want to. In 1789, when he was recalled from Paris to become Washington's Secretary of State, he wrote, "If I could not go to heaven but with a party, I would not go there at all."[2]

But he did organize a political party by doing what Hamilton, Adams, and the Federalists would not do — proselytize among the voters. With letters and visits he and Madison rounded up and organized their supporters. Virginia was the base of operations. But that state, big, powerful and proud, could not deliver the Union. Discontent in the North had to be rallied to the Anti-Federalist, or — as it soon came to be called — the Republican side. In 1791, Jefferson and Madison made a "botanizing" expedition into New York, Hamilton's home state. They won the support of the political outs, led by Governor George Clinton. These were a faction who were not profiting from Hamilton's fiscal policies.

There were similar visits and a flood of letters to other states. Promises were exchanged and the malcontents of the South and North were organized in support of Jefferson.

Today the Democratic party traces its origins to Jefferson. Maybe. It is more likely that Jefferson's was a separate party and the Democrats originated with Andrew Jackson. If there is any basis for the Democratic party's claim it is this: New York Governor Clinton and his lieutenant Aaron Burr transformed a New York City benevolent society known as the "Sons of St. Tammany" into Tammany Hall, the seat of the Democratic political organization in the metropolis for well over a hundred and fifty years. Jefferson formed his Republican party out of an alliance of Tammany Hall, other big city political bosses, and part of the South. That, too, has remained the basic strength of the Democratic party to this day.

For the next step in the development of political parties, twenty-eight years must elapse. The Republicans had remained in power through a Virginia dynasty of Jefferson, Madison, Monroe, then John Quincy Adams of Massachusetts. It was a case of presidents picking their successors, usually elevating a member of their cabinet. With the Federalists dead, the Republican party remained, through the "Era of Good Feeling," the only political party in America.

But a form of revolution was brewing. Property qualifications for voting were being discarded, particularly in the West. Simple, ordinary men, newly enfranchised, were clamoring for a voice in government. They captured state legislatures and sought power in Washington.

That which the Founding Fathers had feared and sought to prevent was occurring. The dominant political power in the country was vested, not in the well-born, the educated, and the wealthy, but in the poor and near-poor, the uneducated, and the men of humble origins. A whole new class of political leader emerged, typified by Martin Van Buren of New York and James Buchanan of

Pennsylvania, both of whom became president. Born in poverty, they rose through politics to become national leaders.

The rise to power of masses of common people is the stuff of revolutions, such as the French and Russian revolutions. Indeed, the term has often been applied to the political metamorphosis that occurred in 1828, when Andrew Jackson went to the White House. But as revolutions go it was not much of a one. The common man of the West and the frontier had no thought of taking away the wealth of the rich. He wanted only the opportunity to become rich himself and, for the most part, this meant to him cheap land in the West. He had no idea of upsetting the political system. He simply wanted to use that system to exercise its power. That meant throwing out Easterners and installing Westerners. To borrow an expression from current Vice President Spiro Agnew, the Westerners considered Easterners "effete snobs." They needed to be replaced by the common man.

The "revolution" began locally, then spread to individual states. Its focus was in Tennessee, Kentucky, Ohio, although perhaps no state in the Union was spared at least a little of its influence. The political problem was to find a national leader under whom all the state factions could rally. He was found in Andrew Jackson. He had fought the Creek Nation of Indians and had defeated the British at the Battle of New Orleans in the War of 1812. Tall, rail-thin, "Old Hickory" became a popular hero, worshipped by the Democrats, as members of the new party, succeeding the Republican party, were soon called.

Jackson seemed to epitomize the aspirations of the common man. Born in a log cabin, he had risen to become a famous general, a national celebrity, and a wealthy plantation owner. He was still simple in his tastes, gruff, strong-willed, poorly educated, and extremely distrustful of education and the educated.

Yet Jackson was not really one with the people who swept him into the White House in 1828. When he was inaugurated, he mounted his white horse and rode to the White House. His followers, who had descended on Washington to see their idol, followed him inside. They gawked at the opulence, stood on the silken furniture, spilled the punch, and in general had a grand celebration. Jackson was not around to see it. He fled out a back door to avoid his constituents.

The "Jacksonian Revolution," as the history books call it, became somewhat of a model for other revolutions that followed. Time and again under stress of social change—for example, following the Civil War; in the struggles of the labor movement near the turn of the century; the Great Depression of the 1930s—Americans have rejected Socialism, Communism, and other radical change and chosen to effect change through the existing political system. There is no guarantee it will always be so, but the past is clearly thus.

The Jacksonian Revolution spawned the two-party system. Those who opposed Jackson and the Democrats who followed him formed the Whig party. It was a collection of factions. It never did develop a positive program in opposition to the Democrats. It was held together with the cement of negativism. All that united the Whigs was opposition to the Democrats. Yet it twice elected presidents. Since both died in office, four Whigs sat in the White House: William Henry Harrison and John Tyler from 1841 to 1845 and Zachary Taylor and Millard Fillmore from 1853 to 1857.

The Whig party broke up over the slavery issue. Next, just prior to the Civil War, came the Republican party which exists today. The Republican party began in the Midwest among those opposed to slavery. Its aim and its cement were abolition of slavery. It ran John C. Frémont in 1856 and elected Lincoln in 1860. It remained the dominant party in the United States until the Great Depression and 1932. Its source of strength was business, the middle class, and the farmers. It may, in registered numbers, be the minority party of the two major parties, but it has remained a vigorous one, offering an alternative which Americans have turned to at times. It has controlled Congress for only two years since 1933. Yet it has elected two presidents since then: Dwight Eisenhower, 1953-61, and Richard Nixon, the current president. The Republican party is very much alive.

The Democratic party is little short of amazing in its endurance and resiliency. Founded by Jackson, it largely controlled the nation until 1860. Somehow it survived the Civil War and the loss of the Southern Democrats who seceded into the Confederacy. The Northern Democrats were further split into the peace and war Democrats. But so great was its strength that Lincoln, in his second term, had to take a war Democrat, Andrew Johnson, as his vice presidential running mate. Even during the war, for which the Republicans blamed the Democrats, the party elected several governors, notably in New York. Between 1860 and 1933, the Democrats held the White House for only sixteen years — the two terms of Grover Cleveland and Woodrow Wilson — yet the party survived. It is today the dominant party in the United States in terms of voter registrations and control of Congress.

It would seem that the political party was an immediate solution to the divisive shortcomings of the Constitution. By having only two political parties at a time — and great efforts have been made to keep just two dominant parties — a choice seemed to be offered. The winning party would surely represent a majority of the people and would be free to put its program into action, while accepting the criticisms of the minority party and protecting the liberties of those in dissent.

This is exactly what has happened in those rare periods in which the United States has taken dynamic action to cope with its problems. In 1965, an overwhelmingly Democratic Congress led by a strong Democratic president, who had been elected by the largest majority in history, passed a stunning array of bills of a generally liberal or progressive nature. Some of them had been advocated for decades, but had never been passed. Yet those who opposed — persons generally of a more conservative bent — were neither silenced nor abused. They were simply outvoted.

A half-dozen years later there was still an overwhelmingly Democratic Congress. But now there was a Republican president chosen by an extremely narrow margin. He received only forty-four percent of the vote, because of the vote for George Wallace and scattered votes for small-party candidates. Mr. Nixon proposed several bold, imaginative programs, such as welfare reform and sharing federal revenues with the states, which he believed would be beneficial to the nation. But nothing much happened. The old process of deadlock and drift had returned.

Clearly, there is something about the political party system of the United States which is self-defeating in terms of unity and action. An obvious difficulty is that there are only two major parties. How can only two parties encompass the bewildering economic, social, racial, religious, ethnic, regional variety which is America? It is not a flippancy to answer, "Not very easily." Today as throughout their history, the two political parties have struggled to find candidates and programs which would unite as many of their diverse elements as possible.

There is no point in an elaborate history of these struggles: how the Democrats, for example, found ways to join together the Old South, workers, ethnic minorities, and intellectuals to form the New Deal majorities under Franklin Roosevelt in the 1930s and 1940s. Nor to detail how the Republicans fashioned such a long-time majority by uniting large and small businessmen, the middle class, and farmers. What is important is that the two parties encompass an incomprehensible variety.

What can be said about one party can be said also about the other. Both the Republican and Democratic parties contain conservatives, moderates, and liberals on nearly every issue; those who want and do not want nearly everything; all races; all economic strata. One of the major differences between the two parties is the degree of influence of these various elements. The Democratic party contains large numbers of rich and conservative businessmen, but it has historically been dominated by wage earners, members of racial, religious, and ethnic minorities, and by liberals who support these groups and want changes to benefit them. The Republican party also contains many members of minorities, but it has historically been dominated by businessmen, the middle classes, and those who believe more in individual enterprise than in government action.

Party labels might be more meaningful if the Democrats, for example, threw out all the conservatives and businessmen and became a party of the poor, minority, worker, and liberal, leaving the Republicans to represent businessmen, the affluent, and conservative — or if two new parties were developed along these lines. The British do something like this with their Labour and Conservative parties. But America's parties never have and it is not very conceivable that they ever will.

What is left is two parties trying desperately to mean all things to all people. A conservative Democratic senator such as James O. Eastland of Mississippi finds far more in common ideologically with a conservative Republican such as Senator Barry Goldwater of Arizona, the 1964 presidential nominee, than he does with a Democratic liberal such as Edward Kennedy of Massachusetts, yet Eastland and Kennedy are both Democrats. Liberal Republican Senator Jacob Javits probably finds little to share ideologically with Conservative Senator James Buckley, yet both represent New York. Even more unlikely is the existence of both blacks and race-baiting whites in both parties, although this is historically more a phenomenon of the Democrats.

In recent years the cement that holds such diverse elements together has come unstuck and there have been some celebrated defections. Senator Strom Thurmond of South Carolina, a conservative Democrat, switched to the Republican party. Some years ago Republican Senator Wayne Morse of Oregon declared himself a Democrat. More recently Mayor John V. Lindsay of New York City, a liberal Republican, joined the Democrats.

In so doing, these prominent men did exactly what large numbers of people do every time they enter a voting booth — switch parties. The political parties do not issue a membership card or collect dues. The party candidates talk a great deal about loyalty to party and the evils of the opposite party, but they have no way to hold the allegiance of a single person. About two-thirds of the registered voters in the nation are Democrats; yet it is obvious that large numbers of them voted for Republican Dwight Eisenhower and Richard Nixon for president and for the large numbers of Republican senators, representatives, governors, and other officeholders. Maine is historically a Republican stronghold; yet its Democratic senator, Edmund S. Muskie, is a leading contender for the 1972 Democratic nomination. Such traditionally Republican states as New Hampshire, South Dakota, Wisconsin, Iowa, and Indiana have one and sometimes two Democratic senators.

Such phenomena are in part a product of the traditional independence of the American voter. Ticket splitting is a time-honored art. Ohio, to give one example, managed to elect a Democratic governor and a Republican senator in 1970. There is a hard core of party faithful who can be counted on to vote a straight ticket, either Republican or Democratic, in every or nearly every election. These party faithful are assiduously wooed and praised by party leaders. But the majority of party members bolt their party once in a while, at least, to vote for a member of the opposition whom they know or like or agree with.

Both parties try to hold their diverse elements together by nominating candidates with broad appeal. In a word, they try to nominate moderates for national and statewide offices. A moderate is mortar. He cements together those diverse elements. The liberals and conservatives in the party may not be enthusiastic about him, but they will accept him as tolerable, where they would not one of opposite ideology. Even when a candidate is more liberal or more conservative, he tries to mollify those opposed to his opinions by expressions of sympathy, understanding, or admiration for those who disagree with him. He may not be a moderate but he lets everyone know he believes in moderation.

Another means of gaining party unity, as well as defections from the opposite party, is to say different things to different people. A candidate might be strongly dependent upon the labor vote and doing everything he can to court it, but if he addressed a businessmen's group, such as the Chamber of Commerce, he'd find something about business enterprise to praise. Every national candidate says something different in the heart of Dixie than he does on the sidewalks of New York. In 1968, Richard Nixon effectively used hour-long television panel shows. He did ten of them in different regions in an effort to appeal directly to regional attitudes.

The most important way of maintaining party unity is to avoid the issues that divide, or, failing to avoid them, gloss them over with pious platitudes or glittering generalities. In the 1968 election, ending the Vietnam War was a major issue. Richard Nixon criticized the handling of the war, called for new leadership, said he would provide it and would end the war. But he did not say how. Mr. Nixon also campaigned on a law and order issue, promising to make the streets safe and generally control crime. But he did not say how he would do this difficult task other than by appointing a new Attorney General, which he would do anyhow, since every president appoints his own cabinet members.

It can be accepted that Mr. Nixon had a plan for ending the war. At least, soon after taking office he began to carry out one, first enlarging the war into Cambodia and Laos, then turning over more of the fighting to the South Vietnamese while withdrawing American troops. But, presumably, Mr. Nixon felt that going into such a plan in the campaign would lead only to further disagreement among Republicans and among the Democrats he hoped would vote for him over the war issue.

Mr. Nixon is hardly unique in such tactics. Every candidate does it most of the time. Only rarely does a candidate for a national or statewide office take a forthright stand on a controversial public issue. He renders generalities. He is for better education, full employment, full production, lower taxes, lower prices, law and order, justice for everyone, equality for women, better housing and much, much more. All of these are noncontroversial as *goals*. Nearly all citizens desire them. But each one is exceedingly controversial when it comes to a specific plan to achieve it. It is a simple matter for a candidate to be for a cleaner, more beautiful America, for example, yet avoid a specific anti-pollution program.

There are a few issues that nearly every candidate can speak about forthrightly—those which nearly all Americans agree about. Some are opposition to Communism, dangers of the Communist menace, peace, a strong national defense to maintain the peace.

The need for cement for the disunited parties, the avoidance of meaningful discussion of the issues in the name of unity or belief that voters are disinterested tend to create campaigns based upon personalities. Every effort is expended to choose candidates on such bases as handsomeness, lovely family, articulateness, vigorousness, friendliness, genuineness, intelligence, and the general impression he makes in the family living rooms as seen on television. Republicans and Democrats might disagree on the issues that divide them, but they can agree that their candidate is photogenic and forceful.

All of this applies, as has been emphasized repeatedly, to national and statewide candidates. Mayoralty candidates in large cities might also be chosen by their parties in a similar manner. But such large-district candidates are the smallest part of politics in America. To understand the rest and its importance, we must take up the organizational structure of the political parties.

5

Politics — Main Street U.S.A.

IN MAY 1832, leaders of the Democratic party (it was then called the Democratic-Republican party) met in Baltimore, Maryland, to choose nominees for president and vice president. In truth, they assembled to choose a nominee for vice president. Andrew Jackson could have been nominated for a second term as president by acclamation. But there was disagreement whether Vice President John C. Calhoun should be re-nominated or Secretary of State Martin Van Buren chosen. The delegates met, argued, and voted for Van Buren to run with Jackson.

The Democratic National Convention has been meeting every four years ever since, making it one of the most enduring political institutions in the world. The Whig party quickly adopted a similar system. Later, the

Republican party came to use essentially the same methods. Not much change has occurred. The 1972 presidential nominees will be chosen in conventions in San Diego (for the Republicans) and Miami (for the Democrats) in a manner not significantly different from that used to choose Jackson and Van Buren.

After 1832, there were a few further developments in the organization of the Democratic party, but by 1850 it had been organized along the lines it still has today. When the Republican party came into existence, it organized itself about the same as the Democrats. There has been no essential change since 1850. The only alteration has been the creation of a parallel organization for women party members.

There is no need here to itemize the changes which have occurred in transportation, communication, the economy, education, general attitudes and life in America since 1850. Yet, the apparatus of political parties remains essentially the same as it was a century and a quarter ago. We have a political horse and buggy to which has been appended radio, television, and other means of mass communication, the jet and other forms of modern transporation, advertising, public relations and marketing techniques—but the horse and buggy still plugs along.

Anyone who wishes to understand the role of the political party in The System must comprehend the extremely *local* nature of American politics. Appearances are deceiving. The newspapers, news magazines, and television newscasters dwell almost exclusively on national politics. Americans are told constantly about the president and presidential hopefuls. We hear about senators and an occasional representative, such as the Speaker of the House or a committee chairman who reaches the spotlight for a moment. At election time, newspapers mention candidates for state governor (gubernatorial candidates) and in rare instances a mayoralty election in a large city. All of these are important, but all is window dressing. It is not real politics. It is not where The System operates.

Real politics is almost entirely local politics, a condition positively guaranteed by the organizational structures of the political parties.[1]

The basic unit is the *precinct*. It consists of a few hundred or a few thousand voters living in a neighborhood. It may be composed of only a couple of city blocks. Its head is a precinct captain, whose responsibility is to control the vote of the party in his area. Depending upon circumstances, he may be asked to get out additional votes or keep from getting them out. He may be asked to recruit other people to the party, or he may be asked to keep the party membership small.

The next unit in size is the *ward*. It consists of many precincts and represents a large section of a city. A village might consist of a single ward with two or three precincts. A small town might have two or three wards. The man in charge for the party is called a ward leader. There may or may not be a district leader. He is usually found in a large city and is responsible for several wards.

Next in size is the county organization. It consists of a committee formed of the various ward and district leaders in the county who elect a chairman. In a large city, such as New York, which includes several counties, there will be several county leaders who may join to form a city committee and elect a head.

This process is not as democratic as it sounds. The county chairman's power stems from his personality and his ability to persuade people, deliver votes, raise funds, and influence the local government. Because of his experience, money, or persuasiveness, he is simply the most powerful man in the party in the county. He may be an elected official, such as a mayor or United States senator. He may be entirely unknown to the public. He may be weak or strong; that is, able to deliver the county for his party or he may fail in the task consistently. He may have power only in local affairs or he may have great national influence, as does Mayor Richard Daley of Chicago in the Democratic party.

A state central committee is elected or chosen. It consists largely of county chairmen and other prominent members of the party. It elects a state chairman and also a national committeeman, who may or may not be the same person. The national committeeman is a member of the party's National Committee and sits in on all of its deliberations. The chairman of the National Committee—Senator Robert Dole of Kansas for the Republicans, and Lawrence O'Brien for the Democrats, at this writing—are at least the nominal leaders of the party nationally.

The national, state, and sometimes a large county committee will organize themselves into smaller units, such as a finance committee for fund raising, a platform committee for drafting the party's principles and programs, a registration committee to get people to the polls, and others.

The Constitution may make no provision for political parties, but the parties are deeply entrenched in the law. Indeed, the two-party system in the United States is a fixture of the law; that is, local and state laws. Elections are conducted, by law, by some form of elections board. It consists of an odd (that is, not an even) number of individuals. The majority represent the party, either Democratic or Republican, that won in the last election. The minority are from the losing party. The board is empowered by law to register voters, print ballots, operate polling places, and otherwise see that the election occurs in accordance with the law.

A similar division occurs in precinct polling places. Each party is represented by judges and other officials. Each party is watched by the other to see that only duly registered voters are permitted to vote and that no hanky-panky occurs. A certain amount does, but in the main Americans conduct amazingly honest elections, simply because of the presence of both parties in the polling places.

Who are these local political chieftains? The classic image is of a somewhat obese man, sweating profusely, and chomping on a long cigar, wallowing in corruption, self-interest, and duplicity. Some people of that sort exist. But some are also intelligent, able, experienced, and dedicated to the welfare of their communities and the nation. Their ranks include lawyers, businessmen, public-spirited volunteers, the naive, and the cynical — a full spectrum of American life.

But the most able of them are professionals; that is, they derive their income from politics or they devote so much time to it that they live and breathe it. They have served a long apprenticeship, coming up through the precincts, wards, districts, and counties. They are extremely experienced in political techniques and thoroughly knowledgeable about the voting patterns in their district. They are nothing if they are not practical, and that which is practical is *power*.

It is said all men are motivated by money, power, or glory. Most men in politics are power men. They need to be able to control or influence other men, whether above or below them. In practical terms, power means being able to pick a nominee, raise money, and deliver votes in a district. If he cannot do this on a fairly consistent basis, the incumbent is out and someone else has power.

Prior to the New Deal in the 1930s, and the passage of the welfare, unemployment compensation, social security, and other such laws, local political leaders could control the vote by passing out baskets of food, providing a load of coal, or finding jobs for voters in their areas. The government does this today, but political leaders are not at a loss. They do favors. They fix tickets, have a traffic light installed, ask a leading officeholder to cut a ribbon to open a store, arrange for a policeman to direct traffic at a church bazaar or even a private party, see that the snow is shoveled regularly on certain streets, arrange appointments with the mayor or have him attend a benefit or private party for a few moments. People appreciate these favors as much as they did a basket of fruit or a bushel of coal in the old days. The political

leader is basically working the same old stand he did in
Andrew Jackson's day.

To understand politics in America it is necessary to
grasp a simple fact: the smaller the political office the
greater its importance to the political leader.

A ward, district, or county leader, although he may
insist otherwise, is not terribly concerned about who the
president is. Oh, he cares, much as any other citizen
cares. The leader is patriotic and interested in his country and its progress. If the local leader backs the right
man and he becomes president, that improves the leader's influence. Everyone realizes how smart he is and
there are mutterings about his influence at the White
House. But as a practical matter, the president doesn't
do very much to ease the problems of the local leader in
controlling local politics.

A senator or representative is nice, for they enhance
his influence in the same way. The local leader can pre-
tend to have influence because he is on a first-name basis
with the man in Washington. The men in Congress and
the president can make his local tasks easier by making
the economy healthy so there are jobs and prosperity. The
local leader benefits, if he is a member of the party
which performed these miracles, because voters are
more sympathetic to that party.

But none of these glamorous national officials — unless
they happen to be important political bosses in their own
right — can do what is truly important to the local leader.
They cannot give him a majority on the elections board.
They cannot get a liquor license issued to an important
contributor of campaign funds. They cannot put the cop
out in front to direct traffic, install a traffic light, issue a

parade permit, hire new workers at the water treatment plant, build a new school—or anything that contributes to the skein of favors, jobs, and influence which elects local officials.

A governor can do these things. A state legislator can do more. A mayor can do still more. And a city councilman can do the whole lot. In rural politics the county leader would trade ten federal officeholders for one good county commissioner.

To repeat: politics in America is local politics.

Those who would understand The System must grasp another simple fact: the local political leader would like to but he doesn't *have* to win the general election in November to stay in power. What he must do is control the nominations. If he fails to do this he is out of power. He can lose election after election, but if he can nominate, power is his.

How does the political leader control the nominations? He does it through the primary election. Nearly every candidate for any office, other than president, stands for election in a primary. This is an election normally held in the Spring. Members of a party, Democrats or Republicans, vote for the men they wish to be the party nominees for various offices. The elected men run against the nominee of the other party in the general election in November.

Primaries, in all but exceptional cases, are dull, desultory affairs. The candidates make speeches and campaign, but the political leaders of both parties work rather hard at not whipping up much enthusiasm for anyone. The local leaders of both parties in all election districts are counting—desperately—on a small voter turnout, on the order of 20 or 30 percent of the eligible voters. If they got 50, 75, or 90 percent of the registered members of the party at the polls in a primary it would upset the leaders' applecarts in a very large manner, for all those good people wouldn't know whom they were *supposed* to vote for.

The key man is the precinct captain. If he is good at his job, he knows everyone in his district. He knows whom they voted for in the last election. He knows to which party they belong. He knows whether they vote a straight party ticket or whether they are ticket splitters.

The process can be reduced to simple arithmetic for a precinct captain.[2] Say there are 1,000 registered members of the party in his precinct. By a little study of voting records, he knows that at best only 300 of them ever vote in primaries. That means he must deliver only 151 votes to elect the nominee he, the ward leader, or county leader want. It is a rather simple matter for the precinct captain to call upon 151 faithful members of the party and make sure they reach the polls.

In a pinch the precinct captain might have to ingratiate himself to a few people with favors, but if he is any good at his job he has done that already. He simply calls upon them. That act alone reminds them of the favors he has done. When he urges them to be sure to vote in the primary and describes the sterling qualities of his candidate, these favor-receivers get the message.

To remain in power, the political leader must control the primaries for the local offices. If he does not, he will quickly lose his power to the man who can deliver votes and thus nominate the men who will run in the general election. If the leader of a county, say, can control the primaries, any man who wishes to reach the general election must ingratiate himself with, have the support of, and be faithful to that leader. Even if that man bolts the regular political organization, runs as a reform or independent candidate, denouncing boss rule, and is elected, one of two things will happen: he will make peace with the regular leader, enlisting his support in the future, or he will set up a rival organization and force the older leader out. In any event he needs *some* organizational support in the future.

The old-time political boss, storied in books and movies, could routinely select and elect a mayor, governor, congressman, or senator. He had a great deal to say about who became president. This sort of power still exists, although it is far less common. Even where it exists it is handled differently. The boss either selects or supports candidates for city-wide or statewide offices who have voter appeal, such as handsomeness, ability to use television successfully, knowledge of the issues, or whatever. The boss supports this man with funds. He gets out the vote in his behalf in essentially the same old ways, while making generous use of the new techniques of television, advertising, image building, and marketing. The new boss has adjusted to the times. But the result is the same. The candidate, if elected, is indebted to the political boss and likely to follow his advice, suggestions, and maybe commands.

It is increasingly difficult, however, for the political leader to control candidates for large-city mayor, governor, or senator. Routinely these days, attractive candidates who either have money or can raise money run for these offices. They set up an organization of volunteers, if only a temporary one, hire advertising and public relations men, then spend large sums of money on advertising, especially on television. If they can appeal to and enthuse enough voters in primary and general elections they do not need the old-line precinct organization. Television has made it possible for city-wide and statewide candidates to reach into the homes of voters. Such candidates are no longer dependent upon the precinct work er for information about them.

There are exceptions. Television and high-pressure advertising are next to useless for the small district office holder. Only a few congressmen from small districts use television very extensively. It would be useless for the mayor of a small city and all state legislators, city councilmen, judges, and other such office seekers to do so. Television is like a shotgun blast going into all the homes over a state or multi-state area. It would be ridiculously expensive for a candidate for a minor office to advertise in the homes of a large number of people who do not live in his district.

Most such officeholders depend upon traditional means: party organizations, speeches and other campaign appearances, and printed advertisements which can be mailed or placed in local newspapers.

There is one other office in the United States still dependent upon old-fashioned political organizations — the presidency of the United States. The president is still nominated as Andrew Jackson was, by a national convention of party leaders assembled every four years.

6

Electing a President

SOMEHOW IT IS incongruous and somewhat frightening in this age of television and jet planes to think of a convention of ward leaders, county chairmen, and state leaders, their friends and relatives, large campaign contributors, and minor officeholders gathering in some large city in the heat of every fourth summer, amid an aura of hoopla and merrymaking, to select the leader of the most powerful nation in the world — indeed, the leader of the free world. It seems so terribly out-of-touch with the times.

It is perhaps safe to say that large numbers of Americans are either disgusted or bored with the national nominating conventions. In the history books, the conventions are storied and filled with high drama: William Jennings Bryan electrifying the convention with his

"Cross of Gold" speech; a deadlocked convention requiring forty or fifty ballots to choose a candidate. But
when television began to cover the conventions as a
regular event, the American people saw them as a per-
petual yawn, filled with aimless movement, windy
speeches to which no one listened, an incessant rapping
of a gavel to gain attention which few gave, grown men
and women wearing silly hats and waving frantically to
the folks back home, if the television camera happened
to be on them, and disgusting demonstrations for the
candidates by hired performers. This is what the conventions had always been. When large numbers of Americans saw a convention, they were, to use the popular
parlance, turned off.

There is a great deal of virtue to the nominating convention. It will probably remain in America for a long
time, if only because of the difficulty of thinking of
something to replace it. But the virtues of the convention have been lost on television.

Every large convention of whatever group appears to
be and often is noisy, aimless, and windy. If NBC,
CBS, and ABC gave the same minute-by-minute coverage to the annual convention of the American Medical
Association, we would all decide that doctors are foolish
men and stop trusting them. I suspect that if similar television coverage were given to the conventions of the
American Legion or the AFL-CIO, Americans would
conclude that the Democratic and Republican national
conventions are models of decorum and serious purpose.

Television exaggerates the weaknesses of the convention. By showing all, it destroys. There is no point to the

broadcasting of the traditional, but meaningless, second-
ing speeches for a candidate; the enthusiasms of the delegates; the expressions of regard, well meant or phony,
of the host governor, the mayor of the city, and innumerable party faithful. All of this is window dressing, a
fillip, a mirage which conceals what is seriously going on.

Television announcers at the convention feel driven,
both by competition with the other networks and by
their own egos, to search for the scoop, to be the first to
cover that dramatic moment when the convention turns
around and does the unexpected — or to discover a single
moment when the unrelenting boredom of the television
screen might be relieved.

Americans must differentiate, I believe, between television coverage of a convention and the convention itself. It may be disorganized, but it is not aimless. It may
be windy, but it is not frivolous. The conventions have a
long history. It is quite possible to talk about their mistakes. Nominating conventions produced Rutherford B.
Hayes and Warren G. Harding as well as a host of defeated candidates lost to all but the driest history books.
But the nominating conventions also discovered relatively unknown men such as Abraham Lincoln, Theodore Roosevelt, Woodrow Wilson.

In recent times the conventions have produced outstanding men in both parties who would never otherwise
have had the chance for national leadership. A few of
these names are worth remembering by those who scoff
at the conventions. In 1932, Franklin D. Roosevelt was
governor of New York, but he was thought to have only
a remote chance for the nomination. The convention

thought otherwise and named him on the fourth ballot. In 1952 and again in 1956, the Democrats nominated Adlai Stevenson. He was governor of Illinois in 1952, but virtually unknown nationally. He never became president, but he served the nation with distinction and brought a new dimension of wit, elegance, and thoughtfulness to presidential politics. John F. Kennedy rose to prominence in the 1956 Democratic convention, as did, in the 1968 convention, Edmund Muskie, the current front runner for the 1972 nomination.

The Republicans have done as well. In 1940, the Grand Old Party nominated a total unknown, Wendell Willkie. He had never been in politics before. He lost, but he contributed the concept of one world which Americans are still striving for today. Thomas E. Dewey was a relatively obscure New York City prosecutor when he was nominated by the GOP in 1944. He lost that year and again in 1948, but he remained a power in national affairs until a few years before his death in 1971. Dwight Eisenhower and Richard Nixon are products of conventions. Earl Warren was governor of California. Nominated for vice president in 1948, he lost, but his national prominence helped him to be appointed Chief Justice of the Supreme Court with results that are historic.

Many other men who have risen to prominence through the convention process might be named. The point is that something must happen at those seemingly aimless, windy, silly conventions. Someone must deliberate. Some thought must go into the process.

Despite the window dressing, it is well known that

every convention is dominated by a few men, the king-makers who usually choose the nominee. But there have been exceptions. The 1940 Republican convention was stampeded by the galleries. The public in the balconies was swept with enthusiasm for Willkie and forced the delegates to go along. The kingmakers try to prevent that today by controlling those who get seats in the convention, dividing the seats among the supporters of the various candidates.

Reporters on both television and in newspapers know who the kingmakers are. They are the heads of large state delegations, powerful governors and senators, large city political bosses. They are the ones who will decide, and they will decide in such a way that the precinct captains, ward leaders, county chairmen, the plumbers and the housewives, the butchers and the corporation executives, who are delegates, will be enthusiastic about their choice. The reporters also know that even if they get to these kingmakers to ask them a question, these men aren't going to tell them anything. It is a study in the most ludicrous futility for a television announcer to shove a microphone in the face of a major party leader and ask him who is going to win. He will probably answer something like "the best man" or "the convention's choice."

Choosing a candidate is at best a difficult task. Except when an incumbent president is being re-nominated, there will be several candidates of equal appeal. They will have support among the ideological and regional groups which divide the party. The aim is to find a candidate acceptable to the largest segment of the party, as well as one likely to win the general election. Members of the various delegations want to meet the candidates, discuss local issues with him in private so that undecided or wavering delegates can make up their minds.

In many cases the convention is the culmination of months of horse trading. If the choice among candidates is close, local and state leaders want to get something in return for their votes. A state delegation may trade its votes for a vice presidency, a cabinet appointment, a judgeship or some other post in government. The delegation may be won by such a simple thing as a promise to campaign in a state or city, thus aiding local party candidates. Deals of this sort are frowned upon. They are not usually made public and if they become known they are denied. But they happen.

At its worst the nominating convention is a form of party fratricide. Animosities build up within the party and erupt. A process of political backbiting goes on among the candidates and kingmakers until the convention is deadlocked. After repeated ballots the prize is awarded to a less well-known or less highly regarded candidate — the dark horse. The convention goes home, the delegates dispirited, the party tragically disunited.

Or the cement of party unity crumbles over some issue. The disagreements the party has glossed over for years suddenly break into the open. Old hatreds reappear. This happened to the Republican party in 1964. The conservative wing of the party, always powerful, had long given in to the moderate and liberal wings. That year it erupted, and handed the nomination to Barry

Goldwater, refusing to make peace with moderates or liberals. The party was badly split. Mr. Goldwater lost. The Democrats' turn came four years later. Tempers flared over the war in Vietnam and the race issue. Aggravating both were the riots between peace demonstrators and Chicago police, as well as the siege-like security precautions which Mayor Daley had taken to keep the demonstrators from the convention floor. There was name-calling. Insults were hurled. Delegates were arrested. The business of the convention was lost in verbal fights over race and peace. The convention left the party with raw wounds of hatred and disunity. The nominee, Hubert Humphrey, lost.

It is difficult to judge the convention system as a means of nominating two men, one of whom will become president. There are glaring weaknesses. People attuned to extremely local problems are selecting a man to cope with radically different national and international problems. The convention is an assembly of men and women and thereby susceptible to emotion, crowd or even mob hysteria, and impulse. Some extremely inferior men have been nominated and a few elected. Only other safeguards of The System prevented disaster.

On the other hand, the people who gather in the convention are at least interested in and knowledgeable about politics and political issues. They are certainly a far better lot than an assembly of people deliberating on the basis of ignorance, passion, and prejudice. They may even be better than a group of outstanding college professors and other knowledgeable men. Such a group might select a man of knowledge and administrative ability, but if he lacked the political ability to appeal to the mass of people and inspire their confidence, he would truly be a disaster. Furthermore, the conventions have nominated some outstanding men.

Surely there is a better system, but the problem is to think of one. One method, already tried and discarded, was to have the members of Congress select the candidates. All the early presidents, from John Adams to John Quincy Adams, were nominated by members of their party in Congress, as were their opponents. The method was discarded because it made the president, designed by the Founding Fathers to be independent, subservient to Congress. It also was undemocratic, giving the people no voice in choosing the nominees. The rise of Jackson and the nominating convention was a rebellion against the congressional caucus method.

Another technique, already widely used, is to sew up the nomination prior to the convention, reducing the convention's role to the task of ratifying what has already been decided and waiting to see whom the nominee chooses as his vice presidential running mate. Every candidate tries to do this, but few are as successful as Richard Nixon in 1968.

He performed one of the most remarkable acts of political resurrection in history. He had been a representative from California, a United States senator, then vice president under Eisenhower for eight years. Then he ran for president in 1960 against John F. Kennedy, losing by the smallest margin in history. Two years later, Mr. Nixon ran for governor of California and went down to

an ignoble defeat. Everyone, including Mr. Nixon himself, believed he was politically as extinct as the passenger pigeon. In 1968, he was nominated for president by
the Republican party. How did he do it?

For years, while Democrats Kennedy and Lyndon
Johnson were in the White House, he tirelessly courted
Republican county leaders. With an iron constitution
and a stomach that must be renowned, he attended local
party functions, eating innumerable box lunches and
warmed-over turkey dinners. He campaigned for local
candidates. He lent his name and national glamour to
local fund-raising efforts. He shook hands with the party
faithful. He saluted uncountable county and precinct
leaders for their statesmanship and perspicacity. He portrayed himself as a man of moderation of a somewhat
conservative bent. He was a man who could unite the
diverse elements of the party. He also took advantage of
his personality. By all accounts Mr. Nixon is at his best
in small groups, affecting people with his warmth, genuineness and reasonableness. In large groups or on television, he tends to be somewhat stiff, formal, and artificial. Years of courting local party leaders enabled him
to be seen at his best, liked and admired.

As a result, the local leaders came to love him far
more than they had as vice president. He was helping
them to raise funds, to gain stature in the party, to win
local elections, to cement control over the local organization.

Mr. Nixon had one more problem to overcome. He
had to prove that he was still a vote-getter, that is, that
large numbers of individual voters would cast ballots for

him. This he did by entering a large number of Presidential Preference Primaries in individual states. But here all his work with local leaders paid off. The precinct, ward, and county leaders — returning favor for favor — worked for him in these primaries. They got out a pro-Nixon vote and he won them all.

When the Republican National Committee met in Miami the result was a foregone conclusion. The delegates to the Republican national convention were precisely those ward, county, and state leaders or men and women loyal to them whom Mr. Nixon had wooed for so many years. He had proved with their help that he was still a vote-getter. The rest was easy. There were "boomlets" in the press and on television for Governors Nelson Rockefeller of New York and Ronald Reagan of California but the convention might as well not have met. Nixon had it sewed up, because he had played *local* politics for all those years.

Another method, now in use in about half the states, is to have the members of the party in those states select delegates to the nominating convention pledged to vote for the candidate winning a Presidential Preferential Primary in the state.

Much is wrong with the system. It vastly extends the campaign period, from a few weeks in the Fall to most of an election year. The candidates become exhausted. A great deal of money is spent. The voters become bored with the faces and words of the various candidates. In only a few states are the delegates bound to vote for the primary winner. In others the delegates are bound only on the first ballot. The result is not much different from the convention system without the primaries. If one man wins all the party primaries, as Mr. Nixon did in 1968, fine. But if several men win, or if a leading candidate refuses to enter them, the convention is left with essentially the same problem it would have had if the primaries had not been held. For the most part, as presently set up, they are a waste of time and money.[1]

Another possibility is to eliminate the convention entirely and have a nationwide direct presidential primary election to choose the party nominees. Such a system, while surely democratic, would pose some immense difficulties. There would be a dozen or more candidates in the field, including many state governors and senators running as favorite sons. The election would be held in the Spring of an election year with the sort of massive television campaigning that is now done prior to the November general election. In many instances, no one candidate would receive a majority of the primary votes of his party. There would then have to be a second run-off election among the two or three most popular candidates, preceded by a morass of political deals with favorite sons and other state political leaders. The certain result of such a system would be a year or more of nearly incessant political campaigning. There would be no greater discussion of the issues. Candidates would be selected on the basis of television personality and money spent on advertising. All would be a tremendous magnification of what is already a considerable problem in American politics. The nation, not to mention the candidates, would end up exhausted. The expenditures would be horrendous. And there would be great danger in such a system. Hitler rose to power in Germany in the 1930s after the nation perpetrated a series of exhausting elections in search of a majority party.

The convention system takes on virtue in light of the possible alternatives. In any event the convention system is now wedded to the Electoral College system of electing presidents — of which more in a moment. It is eminently possible, however, to avoid discarding the convention system by simply reforming it.

In recent years, both parties have made serious efforts in this direction, but it is especially noticeable in the Democratic party, perhaps because it has a wider range of divisions and more need for cement. Both parties have made a number of reforms and there is great agitation for still other improvements.

The crux of the reform movement is a better method of selecting delegates. The aim is to have the nominating conventions more truly represent the opinions and aspirations of the rank and file members of the party, and to select more intelligent, public-spirited, and fair-minded delegates. The effect would be to reduce the power of the "kingmakers." It might also lead to the selection of presidential nominees who are more representative of the entire party, freer of political control by local bosses, or, at least, more willing to listen to various minority elements in the parties.

Historically, none of this was so. Delegates were largely hand-picked by either the most powerful political leader in a state (such as a governor, senator, mayor or other boss) or by a group of such leaders. To be sure, there was a formality of electing these delegates by either the state central committee, a state party convention, or even a preference primary. But in all instances the powerful political leaders of the state could control the selection of the men and women to be delegates.

If this is doubted, simply ask yourself or any knowledgeable person you know to name five members of the state delegation at the last convention. Informed people may recognize the state governor or a senator or prominent congressman, but the rest might as well all be named "Mac." In addition, many voters are unaware that they are not casting ballots for the actual presidential candidate but instead for a list of unknown delegates pledged to vote for their man at the nominating convention. These pledged people were chosen either by the candidate himself or by local political leaders who like the candidate. They may even have been selected by state leaders who detest the particular candidate. These leaders know that if the time comes in the convention when it is clear the candidate no longer has a chance to win, his delegates will be free to vote for someone else. The astute political leader simply prepares himself for that moment at the convention.

Thus, even the Presidential Preference Primary — along with its other abuses — does not guarantee that the delegates to the convention will be representative of the various factions of the party. Recent history is studded with many illustrations of this. In 1968, Democratic Senator Eugene McCarthy campaigned in many primaries and proved himself to be a popular candidate with a large following in the party. But he was never able to convince state and local political leaders that he was qualified to be president or had any chance of winning. In a word, they didn't like him. Despite all his efforts, he came to the convention with no chance for the nomination and nothing happened to give him a chance. Among the Republicans in 1968, there was abundant evidence that both Governors Ronald Reagan of California and Nelson Rockefeller of New York were highly popular among conservative and liberal elements of the party, respectively. Yet Nixon had the delegates sewed up so that the governors and their supporters might as well have stayed home.

The method of selecting delegates has widened the natural divisions in the parties. Duplicate and rival slates of delegates are sometimes named. This occurs most frequently in states without strong political leadership or where factions of the party are sharply divided. Most famous recent examples were in delegations from Southern states to the Democratic convention. Regular party organizations appointed all white delegations. Democratic blacks chose all black delegations. The issue went to the Credentials Committee of the party. Hearings were held and after long argument and perhaps a fight on the convention floor, a compromise was reached — which pleased no one — seating elements from both factions.

The aim of reformers is to alter the method of selecting delegates so that various factions of the parties are represented — including elements who favor a particular candidate — in a legal and orderly manner.[2]

Two questions must be asked about the reform movement. First, should it occur? If reform were accomplished, the convention might be more representative of the party and its factions, but it might also be hopelessly divided. Divisions might be aggravated. The cement might crumble. There might be a return to the past when forty and fifty ballots were used to nominate a dark horse whom the exhausted delegates could agree upon. Perhaps this would not occur, but it is possible.

Second, if reform is desirable, how is it to be accomplished? At least theoretically, one way would be to have direct election of delegates. They would campaign, making known their views and pledging to support certain issues and candidates. This might work in a sparsely populated state, but in a large state with an immense delegation such chaos would result as to make the notion nonsensical. Besides, the usual small voter turnout in primary elections makes it rather easy, as we have seen, for the local political machine to control the primaries.

A system of proportional representation could be used in those states with presidential primaries. If candidates A, B, and C won, respectively, 50, 30, and 20 percent of the vote, they would be able to name that proportion of the delegates. Something like this happens now rather frequently. The delegation is split, casting, say, $25\frac{1}{2}$ votes for A, 10 for B, $6\frac{1}{2}$ for C, 1 for D.

Another method, which the Democratic party is trying for its 1972 convention and may continue after that, is to have the National Committee establish rules (they are called guidelines) which state central committees or state conventions are to use in selecting delegates. The purpose of the rules is to insure that various factions and candidates are represented and to reduce the ability of local bosses to control the delegations. The party also arranged for examiners to go to various contested states and gather evidence concerning the method of delegate selection. The examiners' reports would then be used by the Credentials Committee in deciding contested delegations.

Politics being politics, the new system has exacerbated party division before it has come into use. Leaders of all factions realized that the chairman of the Credentials Committee, naming the examiners and wielding the gavel, would have great power. Thus occurred, perhaps inevitably, a scrap within the party over the choice of chairman of the Credentials Committee. The old guard of Southerners, labor leaders, and regular state politicians favored Mrs. Patricia Roberts Harris, a lawyer and former ambassador who happens to be black. Reformers led by former Senator Eugene McCarthy and Senators George McGovern and Edmund Muskie favored Senator Harold Hughes of Iowa. There was much politicking and in-fighting before Mrs. Harris won.

Obviously, the reform movement still has a long way to go, but efforts are underway to make the nominating conventions more democratic and representative, less susceptible to boss rule. In terms of the criticisms of The System used in this book, it is an attempt to make the conventions more responsive to public will, offer greater participation to minority groups favoring such matters as Negro rights, peace, urban betterment, environment, and to end the cycle of Tweedle-dum and Tweedle-dee candidates. If the reform works, it could make it easier for large minorities to participate in the selection of a president.

It may be hoped that the convention reforms will work, for it is unlikely that the nominating system can be changed without altering the Electoral College method of electing a president.

The Electoral College, the monstrosity devised by the Founding Fathers, still survives, but it is largely a formality. We have what amounts to direct election of the president by the people, yet the system still has great pitfalls.

The Electoral College functioned as it was supposed to exactly twice, for the two terms of George Washington. He was so beloved that the whole nation could agree on his choice as president.[3]

In 1796, the Federalists nominated, by a process of correspondence and private consultation, John Adams for president and Thomas Pinckney for vice president. Through the same process the Republicans nominated Thomas Jefferson and Aaron Burr. When the electors cast their ballots — the people were still not voting — the results were quite close. Adams got 71 votes, Jefferson 68, which under the Constitution made him vice president. Having your opponent as your second in command was surely less than ideal.

The whole process largely dissolved in the next election, 1800. The Federalists renominated Adams and chose Charles Cotesworth Pinckney for vice president. The Republicans again came up with Jefferson and Burr.

It should be remembered that the Founding Fathers had never specified how the electors were to be chosen.

A major part of the revolution wrought by Jefferson was to have the electors chosen by the people. The people should vote for and then choose electors who were supposedly pledged to vote for either Adams – Pinckney or Jefferson – Burr. Actually, half the electors were chosen by this method and half were named by state legislatures.

Seventy-three Republican and sixty-five Federalist electors were chosen. They duly voted, leaving both Jefferson and Burr with seventy-three votes each. The electors had clearly intended Jefferson to be president, Burr vice president, but the ballots did not differentiate the offices, leaving the two men in a tie. Under the Constitution, the issue went to the House of Representatives. It was so closely divided between the parties that thirty-five ballots were taken during one all-night session before a decision could be reached. Finally, under the leadership of Hamilton, who thought Jefferson a lesser evil than Burr, three Federalist representatives cast blank ballots. Jefferson became president.

As a result of this election, the twelfth amendment to the Constitution was passed. It has the electors vote on separate ballots for president and vice president to avoid the confusion of the Jefferson – Burr deadlock.

The system launched by Jefferson and the Republicans is that in use today. In 1968, Americans may have cast ballots for Nixon – Agnew or Humphrey – Muskie, but actually they were voting for a slate of unknown electors pledged to vote for these men. The electors still go through a formality of casting their votes. The Senate and House of Representatives still open these ballots, count them, and declare the nominees to have been elected president and vice president.

As a formality, the system does not always work. At various times, individual electors have cast their ballot for someone else. There is today no legal reason why Elector X could not take an independent stance and vote for the man he personally prefers. It happens seldom, but it did happen as recently as 1960. In a close election there is absolutely no reason why a single elector could not cast his vote for a man who had not received a majority of the popular vote in his state.

There is also no way even today to prevent a nominee from receiving a minority of the popular votes and a majority of the electoral votes and thus be elected president. It has happened twice in history. In 1824, Andrew Jackson received a majority of the popular vote, but failed to achieve a majority of the electoral votes. The issue went to the House of Representatives where John Quincy Adams was chosen president. In 1876, Democrat Samuel Tilden received a sizeable majority of the popular votes, yet Rutherford B. Hayes, through Republican machinations which put the election returns of three Southern states into contention, became president.

It is eminently possible today to have a nominee win a majority of the electoral votes and a minority of the popular votes. If a nominee won the eleven largest states — California, New York, Pennsylvania, Illinois, Ohio, Texas, Michigan, New Jersey, Florida, Missouri and Indiana — and just one other state he would have a majority of the electoral votes and be elected president, even though he might have considerably fewer popular votes. This occurs because, as a rule, all of the state's electoral votes go for one nominee, even though his popular vote majority in that state is as small as one vote. In 1960, President Kennedy won all of the electoral votes of Illinois, though he carried the state by less than 10,000 votes.

The United States has had fifteen minority presidents; that is, presidents who did not receive a majority of the votes cast in the election. They had the largest number of popular votes (a plurality) but not a majority of all votes cast. The presidents were John Quincy Adams in 1824, Polk in 1844, Zachary Taylor in 1848, Buchanan in 1856, Lincoln in 1860 (less than 40 percent of the vote), Hayes in 1876, Garfield in 1880, Cleveland in 1884, Benjamin Harrison in 1888, Cleveland in 1892, Wilson in 1912 and 1916, Truman in 1948, Kennedy in 1960, and Nixon in 1968. Thus, one president in three has not been elected by a majority of the people.

This circumstance has usually occurred when a strong third-party candidate entered the field. In 1968, as has been mentioned, George C. Wallace drew off nearly 12 percent of the vote, leaving both Nixon and Humphrey with about 44 percent of the vote each.

Another problem with the Electoral College is that it discourages voter participation. The winner takes all. The man who votes for the "wrong" candidate in effect throws his vote away. Under the electoral system it is not counted at all, leading to a "why bother" attitude. It also encourages the party politicians to try for a light voter turnout in which the party regulars — those who vote consistently for a party's candidate, whoever he is — control the election. If large numbers of independent and undecided voters can be discouraged from voting, these party faithful can deliver the state's electoral vote. The situation exists wherein a light voter turnout in New York and California, say, could offset in electoral votes a heavy vote in a half-dozen small states where feelings for the candidates ran strong. Furthermore, there is a pronounced tendency for nominees to campaign hard in those states with large electoral votes and neglect the small states. Indeed, many experts feel one of the reasons why Nixon lost the 1960 election to Kennedy was his effort to carry out a foolish campaign pledge to campaign in every state. As the campaign was drawing to a close he had to go to far-off, sparsely populated Alaska, with its three electoral votes, while Kennedy was free to campaign in the big states. In 1968, Nixon did not repeat the mistake and won the close election with Humphrey.

For all these reasons many Americans believe the Electoral College must be eliminated from the Constitution. Eventually the United States will again elect a president who did not receive a majority of the popular votes. He will be so unpopular that he will have a difficult time leading the nation.

There are, however, powerful arguments for retaining the electoral system, arguments which keep Congress from passing the necessary Constitutional amendment. Foremost is the belief that the electoral system perpetuates the two-party system in the United States. The winner-takes-all system in the Electoral College means that a third- or fourth-party candidate has virtually no chance of winning. He might campaign hard and win many votes, but carry only a few states. In 1912, the highly popular Theodore Roosevelt ran as a third-party candidate. He won over 27 percent of the vote, more than the regular Republican and incumbent president, William Howard Taft. Yet Roosevelt won only 88 electoral votes. All he accomplished was to elect Woodrow Wilson, who won 41 percent of the popular vote and 435 electoral votes. In 1968, Wallace, with 12 percent of the popular vote, won only 46 electoral votes and could not deny the election to Nixon with 301.

Americans believe that the two-party system is integral to the whole form of government. Indeed, the strong democracies, such as those in the United States, Britain, and other countries of Europe, have only two major parties. Hitler came to power in Germany in the 1930s when fifteen parties were fighting for control of the legislature. France was plagued with unstable government because of the multiplicity of splinter parties until Charles de Gaulle imposed a new constitution making it easier to form a majority party. Italy is victimized by splinter parties, requiring any government to be a coalition of many parties. A unified approach to the nation's problems is extremely difficult.

A second reason for keeping the Electoral College is that it benefits the small states. It will be remembered that representatives are elected by population, but every state is entitled to two senators. Today, five states have only a single representative in the House and another ten states have two representatives.* Clearly, it is more

*See Chapter Eight, page 131 for further details.

difficult in the first five states to be elected a single representative than to be elected as one of two senators. In the latter ten states, the difficulty is equal.

The addition of the two senators gives each of these small states two extra votes in the Electoral College. These fifteen states are given additional importance in electing a president. They more than offset the largest states which have many representatives, but only two senators.

The small states are reluctant to give up these two senatorial votes. They carry extra importance compared to the big states. If the electoral system were abolished, presidential nominees would campaign solely in the large states, ignoring the small ones. But huge votes of the populous states would immerse the small ones. Also, the candidates would seek to garner only the votes of city and suburban residents, ignoring the problems and demands of the rural voters in sparsely populated states.

Congress has wrestled in recent years with several ideas for coping with these problems. They may be summarized as follows:

1. Do nothing. Leave the present system alone. Agreed, it is filled with dangers, minority presidents, a president who received less votes than the man he defeated, an election thrown into the House of Representatives. But in the main the system has worked well for almost two hundred years. A new system might cause greater problems than the one it replaces.

2. Eliminate the electoral system altogether and institute direct election of the president. It would be fairer. It would be more democratic, expressing the will of the people to a greater extent. There is the practical problem

that direct election might encourage splinter candidates. Three, four, or a half-dozen popular candidates would mean that no man received a majority of popular votes. What would happen if there were, say, five candidates and each received about 20 percent of the votes. Whoever won would be so unpopular as to be unable to govern effectively. One proposal is, in the event no candidate received 40 percent of the vote, to have a second, runoff election between the two men receiving the largest number of popular votes. This now occurs in several states, particularly in the South. It would also greatly encumber the election machinery, extend the campaign process, and delay the national decision on the president.

3. A number of prominent senators have urged the adoption of a proportional system, such as is used in France. Instead of one presidential nominee receiving all of a state's electoral votes and his opponent none, they would share them on the basis of the percentage of the popular vote they won. For example, Ohio has 26 electoral votes. In a close election, the electoral votes might be divided 14 and 12 or 15 and 11, instead of 26 and 0. This would cause several problems. It would also encourage splinter parties and probably throw many elections into the House of Representatives because no nominee received a majority of electoral votes. It would make it possible, furthermore, for a nominee to run up a big majority in a few states or even a single state, more than offsetting close elections in other states. For example, if a man won big in New York, he might receive such a large proportion of its electoral vote as to more than offset a narrow victory or loss in California.

4. The district plan. Under this, each state would have the same number of electors it now has. But each elector would represent, not one whole state, but a district or section of territory of approximately equal population. The nominee who won the district would receive one electoral vote. But in the whole state he might win only half the districts or only one. His total nationwide electoral vote would reflect his actual voting strength. This plan would also encourage splinter parties and increase the risk of election by the House of Representatives rather than the people. In addition, there is the problem of fashioning the districts. Who would do it? There is a great risk of gerrymandering; that is, fashioning the districts so as to favor one party over another, which happens regularly in congressional and state elections now. By changing the boundaries to include, say, a lot of Republican voters, it can be made difficult or impossible for a Democrat to win. Needless to say, the Democrats also do this to defeat Republicans. The whole system of gerrymandering, which has existed in America since Colonial times, is highly odoriferous. Many people feel that injecting it into a presidential election would damage the prestige of the office.

7

Politics –
Selling a Cake of Soap

IN THE 1968 general elections, advertising managers for
Richard Nixon's campaign decided to use a type of sixty-second television commercial which utilized still pictures and a voice over. For the uninitiated, which is
most of us, this means a movie camera would photograph still pictures in such a way as to create a feeling
of motion. It is an established technique, frequently used
to re-enact a moment in history which occurred before
the movie camera was invented. While the pictures were
being shown a voice of an unseen person would make a
few remarks. The voice would be that of Mr. Nixon.

The first of eighteen such commercials was on the
Vietnam War. It showed photographs of the war and of
wounded American and Vietnamese soldiers, as well as
their haggard faces. A closing picture was of an Ameri-

can GI marching off to battle with the word "Love" written on his helmet. Over this was Mr. Nixon's voice calling for an end to the war and new leadership toward that aim. He promised to bring an honorable end to the war.

Reaction to the commercial was unfavorable. Some of Mr. Nixon's advisers felt the commercial was somewhat dovish and would have a negative effect in the South and Southwest where the Vietnam War was considered by Mr. Nixon's advisers to be popular. One of Mr. Nixon's managers objected to the word "Love" on the helmet. It seemed to equate the candidate with hippies. The shot was deleted and a photograph of a soldier with a plain helmet inserted.

Later the maker of the commercial received a letter from the mother of the soldier who bore the word "Love" on his helmet. She thought it a wonderful picture of her son and asked if she could have a copy. She signed the letter with her name, Mrs. William Love.

This incident was described by Joe McGinniss in his best-selling book *The Selling of the President 1968.*[1] A person doesn't know whether to laugh or cry over this incident and many others described in the book. There is something pathetically ludicrous about a nominee for the most powerful office in the Western world placing himself in the hands of adverstising managers and television directors to be sold like a cake of soap, a box of breakfast cereal, or a can of beans.

None of this is said as direct or implied criticism of the President. His opponent, Hubert Humphrey, did essentially the same thing. Indeed, every candidate for large-city mayor, governor, senator, or large-district congressman does it.

Mass communication — most particularly, television — poses a most difficult problem for the American political system. Candidates for any office have long advertised. They have had printed flattering pictures, matchbooks, flyers and handouts, newspaper advertisements. In time they learned to make their views and voices known on radio. But all of this pales before the impact of television. The voter sits in his living room and receives both the visual and auditory impression of the man, and of these two the visual, a motion picture, is by far the more important. The eye will react to motion and force the mind to follow what is moving.

Anyone can buy a printed advertisement. If you are a candidate for city councilman, walk into a photographer's studio and have your picture taken. Select the one you believe flatters you the most, makes you look youngest, most vigorous or appealing. Take the photograph to a print shop and arrange to have a large number of copies printed. Or, contact a match book salesman and order 100,000 matchbook covers imprinted with your photograph. With ease you could compose the words for the cover. You might say, "Vote for Better Government, Vote for . . .," whatever your name is. If you wished to advertise in a newspaper, you could telephone and ask for an ad of a certain size and compose the message you wished printed. The newspaper would pick up your picture.

If you wished to advertise on television and had enough money, you could go to the studio, buy a minute or half an hour of time, enter a studio, stand there and make a speech. This was essentially what was done in the late 1940s and early 1950s, the first days of the "boob tube." It was effective in the sense that the man and his voice became visible to a large audience, but it was also boring. Large numbers of viewers went off to raid the refrigerator or switched to a Western.

Television is a medium of entertainment. When it comes to information and serious discussion, the printed word and radio are much more effective. By its very nature, television must stress the visual and action. Most sports are a natural on television, with football especially ideal. In the news field, television is at its best where there is action—riots, disasters, men marching off to battle, astronauts on the moon.

Television, being an action medium, is also terribly fleeting. It is on for hours a day, each image being replaced within a fraction of a second by another. Visual and auditory sensations pile up on the viewer in an unending succession. His ability to absorb becomes dulled. His capacity to be interested is reduced. It might be said that it is not religion that is the opium of the people, as Marx claimed, but television.

Those who prepare advertising for television, understanding the medium as they do, quickly learned and are still learning to cope with its advantages and disadvantages. They learned to make commercials mostly visual and only secondarily auditory, entertaining if only through use of the bizarre, extremely short, and—one more thing—emotional. They learned to *involve* the viewer. Buying detergents is not an exercise in cleanliness. It is an emotional experience. To produce a sheet that is anything less than brilliantly white is to lose your womanhood, not to mention husband, children, and friends.

Inevitably, television advertising men and politicians discovered each other. The candidate said, in effect, "If you can sell soap, sell me" and the rest is history, visible on the television screen in any election campaign. Even the most honest, forthright, sensible, and public-spirited of candidates gave themselves over to TV ad men so they could perform their magic tricks.

It is not surprising that ad men would sell candidates as they sell underarm deodorants. Briefly stated, the process begins with a market survey to discover what people think of the candidate. What do they know of him? What do they like and dislike about him? An advertising campaign is developed to improve the unfavorable impressions while enhancing the favorable ones. He is shown only in the best circumstances in which the lighting is perfect, the setting ideal, the camera angles carefully plotted. If he is not especially photogenic or effective on camera, he need not be shown at all; instead, his voice will be heard over still or motion pictures.

America is shown only parts of a man — a smile, practiced gestures, vigorously delivered but meaningless words written by someone else. In a word, we are shown an *image*. We know, because of television and other manifestations of the advertiser's art, next to nothing about the *man*. We are shown pictures of him and his happy, smiling family. Does he fight with his wife? Do his children never aggravate him? Does he never have problems with them? And how does he handle them? Does he have a temper? How does he show it and

how well does he control it? How does he reach decisions? By listening to others, seeking information and
advice? Or is he impulsive, headstrong, and stubborn?
Does he have the capacity to learn? Or does he believe
he already knows it all, feel a compulsion to instruct
others, so that he cannot listen? These and a thousand
other essential human qualities in a national and world
leader are never revealed, unless smiles, gestures, happy
family photographs, and image-building reveal them.
They do not.

The entire nature of modern campaigning is to conceal the detrimental and enhance the good. Americans
are handed a slogan. In 1960 Americans were told,
"Let's get the country moving again," and were shown
an image of young, vigorous John F. Kennedy. We were
not told that he was not especially vigorous physically
because of a back injury, or that he suffered from an
adrenal disease and needed daily shots to cope with
stress. "This time vote like your whole world depended
on it," Mr. Nixon told Americans in 1968. Rather obviously, no politician, not even a president, is that important. But it *sounds* important.

What is so shocking about such techniques is that
they are so disembodied. Advertising and public relations are *techniques*. Sentiment, philosophy, and purpose have nothing very much to do with it. According to
McGinniss one of the men important to Mr. Nixon's
advertising campaign was a rabid supporter of Democrat Eugene McCarthy. No revelation was made of
the politics of Eugene Jones, who produced Mr. Nixon's
spot television commercials. He was paid $110,000
and he did the commercials.

Even when the ad men agree with the candidate and think highly of him, they tend to look upon him as a cake of soap. McGinniss's book contains no more revealing quote than this from one of Mr. Nixon's top ad managers:

> Let's face it, a lot of people think Nixon is dull. Think he's a bore, a pain in the ass. They look at him as the kind of kid who always carried a bookbag. Who was forty-two years old the day he was born. They figure other kids got footballs for Christmas, Nixon got a briefcase and he loved it. He'd always have his homework done and he'd never let you copy.
>
> Now you put him on television, you've got a problem right away. He's a funny looking guy. He looks like somebody hung him in a closet overnight and he jumps out in the morning with his suit all bunched up and starts running around saying, "I want to be President." I mean this is how he strikes some people. That's why these shows are important. To make them forget all that.[2]

The central question is whether this man is putting down the man who became president — or is he putting down himself? In any event, this was a man employed by Mr. Nixon to run his television shows during his 1968 campaign.

No special indictment of television ad men is intended. The whole of modern, large-district campaigning is infused with the concepts of marketing, merchandising, sales, advertising, and public relations.

Professional campaign managers begin by taking a realistic look at their candidate — it doesn't really matter who he is — his strengths and weaknesses. They do the same for his opponent. The object is to accentuate the positive in their candidate and the negative in their opponent.

These matters are usually more complex, but for example's sake, let's suppose that Candidate A is a loyal party regular, while his opponent, B, is a free-thinking maverick. A's managers will promote him as loyal, steadfast, dependable, a man of solid philosophy, a man to be counted on. They will cite him as patriotic, a churchgoer, a family man, a solid citizen embodying the traditional American virtues. B's managers, meanwhile, will show their man as one of intelligence, thought, and independence. He is portrayed as concerned about issues and the voter. A most humane individual he is.

The managers develop images. Candidate A is shown as dignified. The flag is visible in the background on television. He runs on his record, citing his accomplishments while in office. His slogan is, "Vote for good government." Candidate B's managers seek to portray their man as human. He is shown with children in the park or meeting with a group of black teenagers or workers at a construction site. He does not mention his record, but cites the need for change and improvement. His slogan: "Vote for better government."

If the election is close and hard-fought, Candidate A points out that B has no record or a very poor one. B says that his opponent is stodgy, unresponsive to the problems of the voters, and controlled by political bosses.

In a sense, everything everyone said was true. Yet, all dealt in opposites, in extremes. So how can all be true? The only way was for both A and B to deal in partial truths. A man may be a loyal party man, but that does not necessarily make him disinterested and unresponsive. B may be a maverick, but that does not make him less consistent or loyal.

A soap manufacturer develops a detergent that is very good at washing out grease, but has no effect on grass stains. His advertisements show it cleaning grease miraculously. Only after it has been purchased does the housewife discover that it won't clean everything. Something similar happens in politics. Voters are provided with a carefully plotted image, slogans, a theme — and only later discover what other qualities exist.

In his conduct of the presidency, Mr. Nixon has demonstrated a fascination with both secrecy and surprise, much as did his predecessor, Lyndon Johnson. Mr. Nixon showed this in the invasions of Cambodia and Laos and in an abortive raid on a prisoner-of-war camp in North Vietnam. His adviser Henry Kissinger was sent to China amid cloak and dagger secrecy; then the president went on television to reveal a planned trip to confer with Communist Chinese leaders. After many statements saying the nation's economy would right itself, Mr. Nixon did an abrupt about-face, commandeered Sunday night television, and announced a startling new economic program.

The point is not whether these actions were right or wrong, but that they indicate the President's delight in secrecy and surprise. Yet, in his campaigning, Mr. Nixon portrayed himself as dependable and forthright. Nothing in his image suggested the qualities of secrecy and surprise. Perhaps he did not know it himself.

Modern campaigning is rather scientific. Exhaustive analyses are made of voting patterns in past elections.

Not very many years ago I saw the mayor of Baltimore, an experienced politician, read the results of voting in a single precinct and predict the outcome of the election with amazing accuracy. As I recall, he lost. Today such predictions are a fixture on television. Early results are fed into a computer and the victor is forecast. Sometimes only a few thousands or even hundreds of votes have been counted, yet the computer predicts. It is unerring.

How can this happen? It is not at all difficult. A computer is hardly necessary. It is window dressing to make the ordinary look occult. It can be done quite easily with three precincts in a large city. Precinct A has always gone Democratic in the past. If there are 1,000 voters, 750 of them have been Democratic in the past. Precinct B has always gone Republican, casting 750 of its 1,000 votes for the GOP candidate. Precinct C has always been close, with 500 votes going for each party candidate. Great effort is made to count the votes in these three precincts quickly and report them to party headquarters. If A produces 800 Democratic votes, B 700 Republican votes, and C 600 Democratic votes, it is simple to predict a Democratic victory. If the computer programmer wishes to play it safe, he feeds ten or a hundred key precincts into the computer.

This may be magic on television, but it is bread and butter to a political candidate. Let's say a man is a Republican and is running for office in a heavily Democratic city, county, or state. Simple arithmetic tells him the Democratic registration is heavily against him. Therefore, he must hold the regular Republican voters, convince the independent or undecided voters to support him, and get a few of the less stalwart Democrats to switch over to him. His managers know this and they plan his campaign accordingly. He doesn't just run around haphazardly making speeches and shaking hands. All this is planned carefully. He makes a few appearances at the regular Republican precincts and wards. He makes many stops in highly independent districts, and he spends a great deal of time in those districts where Democratic sentiment is believed to be wavering. He simply does not waste his time going to districts where he has no chance.

In 1968, Richard Nixon correctly assumed he had no chance of gaining the black vote. He was also sure to lose the rigidly conservative or racist vote to George Wallace. He had some chance of gaining part of the labor vote. His main source of strength was the suburban vote. Translating this into campaign strategy, he figured to lose the Deep South either to Wallace or the Democrats. Much of the Northeast, especially New York, but possibly Pennsylvania, Connecticut, and Massachusetts were lost. But he should hold the traditionally Republican states of the plains and the Rockies. The key areas were California, Illinois, Indiana, Ohio, and the border states of Maryland, Kentucky, Tennessee, and Missouri. He campaigned in the Northeast and in the Deep South, but most of his effort went into the Midwest and the key states. He won all the key states save Maryland, many by close margins, thus proving the wisdom of his campaign strategy. He wasted scant time in central cities wooing blacks. He spent a great deal of time in the suburbs.

His opponent, Hubert Humphrey, campaigned in central cities and in the Northeast and fought hard for the key, close states.

In political parlance such techniques are known as going where the ducks are. The candidate seeks to keep the votes he has and go after those he can possibly get, ignoring the hopeless. His theme, slogan, advertising, and appearances are aimed at bringing in the votes he needs to win.

The amateur in politics frequently wastes his time trying to convince the unconvincible while neglecting the convincible. He has not done his homework on where the ducks are. Sometimes the most able professional makes similar mistakes. In 1970, Mr. Nixon and Vice President Agnew campaigned vigorously in Texas on behalf of Republican senatorial candidate George Bush. The effect was negative, however. Their appearances stirred up great interest in the election. More voters turned out and most of them were Democrats. Bush lost to Democrat Lloyd Bentsen.

Political campaigning is a subtle art, involving merchandising, advertising, public relations, and cunning analysis of voters and how to motivate them. There is legerdemain. More important than a candidate being sincere is his ability to *seem* sincere on television. More vital than his knowledge of the issues is his ability to seem knowledgeable.

The stakes are high and no effort in advertising or image-building should be left to chance. The candidate may be excellent. He may be sincere. But he must engage in a certain amount of bamboozlement of the voters.

This is the tragedy of American elections. It is very difficult to know what to do about it. It is easy to say that if citizens knew of these techniques they would be on guard against them. But such a statement underestimates the cleverness of ad men. In 1968, Hubert Humphrey, faced with the professional excellence of Mr. Nixon's television appearances, engaged in studied mistakes and haphazardness. On his final pre-election TV show, there were shots of cameras and cables, hopefully intended to lend an aura of naturalness and unstudied innocence.

This is technique. For years Volkswagen in its advertisements has emphasized its smallness, compactness, ugliness, and unchanged styling. It is called "the bug" in advertisements. All is designed to appeal to a form of reverse snobbery, and contrast with the size and expensive styling of American cars.

Years ago, politicians gave up the formal speech on television in favor of informality. A standard format was a visit to the candidate's home and shots of him petting the family dog, romping with the children, and chatting over dinner with his wife. Just a regular guy. This technique was dropped when viewers came to see that the informality was exaggeratedly contrived.

It simply must be assumed that ad men will keep one step ahead of — or no more than one step behind — voters in developing new ways to con them with images, bamboozle, and downright fraud.

The only encouragement is that ad men frequently overestimate themselves. They have an unwarranted enthusiasm for their own ability, and they have worn their ticket thin. Television swarms with advertisements, each one more clever than the last. In a campaign, each candidate, armed with squads of clever ad managers, dulls his own effectiveness by the overabundance of the total effort. And the viewer grows more sophisticated. A child learns that the toy tank on television doesn't really shoot fire. The housewife learns that a white tornado doesn't really come out of a bottle, that her clothes get white whatever soap she uses, and that her neighbor really doesn't reject her for using the wrong soap. So, too, the viewer, faced with two equally handsome, smiling, and genuine candidates, eventually either becomes bored or asks a pertinent question such as "What is he going to *do*?" having heard in abundance what he says. It may be unwarranted optimism, but I believe that eventually voters will reject bamboozlement and insist upon genuineness that is unstudied, honesty that is real, and intelligent discussion of what matters.

Meanwhile, until this millennium arrives, a serious problem results. All of this advertising, travel, and other forms of campaigning costs horrendous sums of money. McGinniss reported that each of Mr. Nixon's sixty-second spot commercials cost $25,000 to produce, besides the cost of the time on television.

It is virtually impossible to discover how much money a large-district candidate spends — if he himself knows — and who provided the money. The state and federal laws requiring the reporting of campaign contributions and expenses are full of loopholes and bear no penalty provisions for incorrect reporting. Many candidates don't even bother to report and many that do make inaccurate or incomplete reports.

Following the 1970 elections, *Time* magazine reported from sources it did not disclose that Governor Nelson Rockefeller of New York spent between $7 and $10 million in winning a new term, while losing senatorial candidate in that state, Richard Ottinger, wasted $3.5 million. Governor Reagan of California invested $2.4 million in winning a new term. *Time* estimated the average cost of running for the House of Representatives was between $40,000 and $70,000 for winner and loser alike. A Senate seat cost $1.5 million per candidate and a governor in a populous state spent at least $1 million. Even in sparsely populated Wyoming (332,000 people) candidates for governor, senator, and the single state representative spent a total of $6 for each vote cast. Where do such sums come from?

Time answered:

> These huge sums, despite the traditional claim of politicians that every dollar came in crumpled bills from the man on the street, are raised from the wealthy few: it is estimated that 90 percent of political funds are donated by 1 percent of the population.[3]

It is obvious that only a wealthy man or a man with wealthy friends and supporters can run for, let alone be elected to, a large district office.

Writing on this matter in 1968, former President Dwight Eisenhower commented:

> In effect, we have put a dollar sign on public service, and today many capable men who would like to run for office simply can't afford to do so. Many believe that politics in our country is already a game exclusively for the affluent. This is not strictly true, yet the fact that we may be approaching that state of affairs is a sad reflection on our elective system.[4]

We have moved perilously close in the United States to a system in which the rich and those who can gain the financial support of the rich can obtain public office in large districts.

Why do people give money to politicians? There are several motives. A few are motivated by a public-spirited belief that the candidate will be very good for the district or for the nation, his opponent very bad. Some simply want flattery. By financing a candidate, particularly if he wins, they can bask in the ability to call him by his first name, get him on the telephone, ask favors, if only attendance at a social gathering at his home. But some have ulterior motives. By providing money, they can control or influence the candidate. They can perhaps persuade him to vote in a desired way. It is a common practice for a large industrialist or a wealthy man of opinion to give money to both candidates in an election, thus insuring influence with the winner, whoever he is.

No candidate is an island unto himself. He must have followers, voters, supporters. Obviously, the more support a man offers, the more his value. No supporter of a candidate would be so stupid as to offer a bribe. He offers advice. He gives an opinion. He seeks to persuade. But behind all the persuasion and advice is money, plain old money.

If the man with the full purse asks an elected office-holder to do something dishonest or something that compromises his principles, the official would not, of course. But the man with the money seldom asks that. He wants only support for a certain issue and offers excellent reasons to support such a view. But in the back of his mind, the candidate knows that if he adopts such an intelligent, rational viewpoint a large check will be forthcoming in the next election campaign.

In 1971, Mr. Nixon announced a program to improve the nation's economy. There were several elements to it, but one was elimination of a 7 percent excise tax on automobiles, a proposed 10 percent tax deduction on capital investments, and a 10 percent surcharge on foreign imports, which include foreign automobiles. It is to be assumed that Mr. Nixon was motivated by a desire to stimulate the economy. The automobile industry is the largest in the nation. When one more automobile is built and sold it not only employs more automobile workers but also additional workers in steel, glass, plastics, aluminum, leather, rubber, and other major industries that supply car manufacturers. The President's program made a great deal of sense and was widely applauded. But it is not cynical to suggest that automobile manufacturers, not to mention the large suppliers, recognized that Mr. Nixon thought correctly by benefiting them. Certainly his campaign managers knew it would be far easier to solicit campaign contributions from automobile manufacturers in the future.

A candidate cares first about votes. Without them, though he have all the money in the world, he is nothing. But—or so it is believed—money can buy votes through the employment of clever advertising and experts in other fields. Money, it is believed, can be translated into votes at the rate of $25,000 a television commercial.

It is axiomatic in politics that he who has money has influence. For generations ambassadorships have gone to large campaign contributors; so have cabinet offices, judgeships, and other appointive positions.

There is nothing inherently evil in money. Many conservative men are wealthy. But so are many liberals. Edward F. Kennedy and his late brothers, President John F. Kennedy and Senator Robert F. Kennedy, were born to wealth so that earning a living was of no concern. Among the Republicans Nelson Rockefeller of New York is extremely rich and also fairly liberal, at least in his concern for minority groups.

Yet there is something inherently wrong in a system that permits money in the form of campaign contributions to unduly influence a political result. It takes a large group of determined voters on a given issue to equal the influence of one significant check.

In 1970, the Democratic Congress passed a measure limiting the amount of money any candidate could spend for advertising in an election to 7 cents for each voter in the previous election. It was widely acclaimed as a reform measure. President Nixon vetoed it, saying a better law was needed, and the bill failed to pass over his veto. Other measures of a similar nature are now before Congress.

Clearly the present system makes it virtually impossible for a poor man or a man of modest means to run for any office more important than congressman from a small district unless he is willing to accept the influence of contributors who supply him money. Equally clearly, some arrangement must be worked out so that the poor or modest can run for public office.

There is no shortage of ideas. One is to stop the purchase of time on radio and television. Broadcasting stations are regulated by the federal government. It could easily require stations to provide a given amount of free time to all candidates during a campaign. Newspapers and outdoor advertisers could be persuaded to do the same. The result would be an end to all paid advertising. All candidates would receive equal space and time.

Another suggestion is for some sort of subsidy to all candidates for their use in campaigning. All candidates would have an equal or pro rata amount.

Another proposal is to put teeth into the laws so that candidates are forced to account for all the money they spend and to report where it comes from.

8

Congress — Whom Does it Represent?

THE LEAST EFFECTIVE branch of the United States government is Congress. It has been so for decades with important repercussions for the American democratic procedure. In recent years leading members of Congress have addressed themselves to the problem, and there have been many studies made on the question of congressional reorganization. Steps have been initiated to correct the deficiency, but nothing of substance has been accomplished, though it must be admitted that congressional reform is a gigantic undertaking.

The ineptness of Congress must be seen in the light of history. The Founding Fathers intended it to be the dominant branch of government. Much of the Constitution creates checks and balances to control the powers granted to Congress, but a simple reading of the Constitution reveals the vast authority vested in the legislative branch. Yet the situation exists today wherein Congress is so ineffective and has been so for so long that it has surrendered most of its powers to the executive and judicial branches. Congress jealously guards what power is left and tries to recover from time to time the powers it has surrendered, but this body, the essence of republican government, remains inefficient, unresponsive, and undemocratic.

One way to point up what is wrong with Congress is to center on just one of its members, the chairman of the House Ways and Means Committee.

This committee has great power in Congress. Under the Constitution, all tax measures must originate in the House, which gives it pre-eminence over the Senate in this field. The Ways and Means Committee has responsibility for all revenue and tax measures, as well as customs, transportation of taxable goods, Social Security, reciprocal trade agreements with other nations, the national debt, and deposits of public moneys. If the power to tax is the power to destroy or if the power to tax is the power to build, it all originates in the Ways and Means Committee.

That is not too strong a statement, for under House rules, the Ways and Means Committee is extremely special. It consists of only 25 members — 15 from the majority party, 10 from the minority, which today means 15 Democrats and 10 Republicans. It meets as a committee of the whole, there being no subcommittees. This gives the chairman, at present Representative Wilbur D. Mills, extraordinary power.[1]

Under House rules legislation reported out of the Ways and Means Committee takes precedence over all other legislation. House rules also specify that the legislation is allowed only two days of debate on the House floor, and that the bill may not be amended on the floor. The bill can only be approved or rejected by the full House.

Mr. Mills rose to his position of power by perfectly ordinary means. He was elected to the House while a very young man in his twenties. Sam Rayburn, then Speaker of the House, that is, the leader for the Democrats, recognized Mills's incisive legal mind and appointed him to the Ways and Means Committee. This was an important appointment, for Rayburn believed that Mills had the capacity to grasp complicated tax matters. He also recognized that Mills came from a safe district; that is, he was likely to be re-elected term after term, thus remaining on the committee and developing his expertise.

That is precisely what happened. Mills was returned to Congress every two years. His seniority grew. Older men died, retired, or were defeated. At age 48 — extremely young — Wilbur Mills was chairman of the Ways and Means Committee. Unless he chose to retire or accept another office, or unless the Republicans gained control of Congress, Mr. Mills was likely to remain chairman for at least a quarter of a century, probably longer. It has thus far happened that way.

In 1970 and 1971, Richard Nixon sought major changes in welfare legislation and in sharing federal revenues with the states. This meant all such legislation originated with Mr. Mills's committee. This gave him tremendous power and a national spotlight.

It also happened that Mr. Mills, through his long tenure on the committee, his experience with many tax matters, and the quality of his mind had won the respect of his colleagues in the House and the Senate. In short, he earned respect for both his position and his ability.

In the summer of 1971, President Nixon offered a new economic program to the nation. Important elements of it had to be approved by Congress. Enter Mr. Mills and his committee. At this point every Democrat thinking of running for president looked to Mr. Mills to perform a miracle; that is, aid the nation's economy, give Mr. Nixon what he wanted, yet put a Democratic stamp on the program so the democratic presidential candidate in 1972 could claim the credit. At this writing every Democrat in Congress is waiting to see what Mr. Mills will come up with. And so is President Nixon.

All this is cited to illustrate a simple fact. Mr. Mills, the most powerful man in Congress when it comes to taxation and related matters, happens to come from Kensett, Arkansas. He is known to be patriotic and public-spirited. He has the interest of the nation at heart. But the plain fact is that he is responsible only to the people of Kensett and environs, the second smallest election district in Congress.

Therein lies a basic problem of Congress. It is an amalgamation of individuals elected in and responsible to individual districts, the largest of which is a single state. The members of Congress have only an ethical responsibility to the United States as a whole. As a practical matter they can do nothing, a little, or a whole lot as long as they please the people in the district that elected them.

Representative Mills, using his great power over taxation, welfare, and social security legislation, might theoretically do something quite useful for the voters of Kensett, Arkansas, but extremely detrimental for the citizens of California and New York, the two most populous states. But if he did, the residents of those two states would not have any right to say anything against him and his power as long as Kensett approved of him and Congress maintained its existing procedures.

In 1971, Congress canceled a contract to build a supersonic airliner. The contract had been placed with the Boeing Company of Seattle, Washington. Cancellation worsened an already bad employment condition in the Seattle area, for men were laid off when work on the airplane stopped. Washington's senators and representatives worked mightily to keep the contract, but they failed.

Many legislators voted against the contract, but Senator William Proxmire of Wisconsin was the leader of those opposing the building of the airplane. He convinced enough senators and representatives of the dangers of pollution from the airplane, the sonic boom it would create, and the lack of need for the high-speed craft to cause its cancellation. The people of Seattle and the State of Washington obviously did not agree with Senator Proxmire, but they could do nothing about defeating him or changing his mind.

On the other hand, suppose a representative from

some large city introduced legislation to stop federal subsidies to the dairy and cheese industries or to greatly increase the taxes on beer — all of which are large industries in Wisconsin. It is quite possible that Mr. Proxmire would feel it necessary to oppose such legislation as wholeheartedly as he opposed a supersonic airplane.

Congress has a great deal of difficulty forming a majority on many issues because its members represent the extremely diverse elements and opinions that exist in the United States. If he wishes to remain in office, a member of the Congress must please the voters of the state or district that elects him. He can be admired for his knowledge, independence, or prominence, but he must also aid the district by creating jobs and favorable economic conditions, erecting buildings, dams, irrigation projects or whatever — in general, make the people of the district feel better off because they have sent him to Washington.

A man from a predominantly agricultural district is expected to advocate and support legislation for farmers. A black congressman or senator will support civil rights, welfare, housing, education, and other legislation of vital interest to black voters. A man from a wealthy "silk stocking" district will take special interest in legislation favorable to the business and financial community.

It is very difficult to get all these people, representing divergent and often polar interests, to agree on anything. There are some ways. Frequently all can agree on subjects of common interest, such as foreign affairs or national defense. But often they engage in elaborate horse-trading. If you will support my farm bill, I will support a new labor law that the people of your district want. If you will support an increase in urban housing, I will vote for a new defense installation in your district. If you will favor a lowered tax on businessmen, I will oppose a gun-control law which your people out West dislike.

Another method is to water down the legislation. I will support this water pollution bill only if it exempts a certain industry important in my state. I will vote for larger income tax deductions for workers, but only if an amendment is added favoring investors and businessmen.

Congress has great difficulty arriving at a majority opinion among all these diverse opinions unless the bill is clearly beneficial (or at least not harmful) to a broad spectrum of the population or unless the problem has gone on so long that a clear majority of the people demand action. To pass legislation that is innovative, to enact bills in advance of a pronounced public awareness of need is extremely difficult.

The problem is worse than that. Congress has great difficulty passing *any* national legislation. In 1970, President Nixon offered to Congress a program to reform the nation's welfare system. The welfare problem is too complex to go into in this book, but suffice it to say the welfare system is inefficient, discriminatory, and wasteful. Large numbers of knowledgeable people have been demanding reform for years. Mr. Nixon and his aides developed a far-reaching reform proposal. The bill lingered in the House Ways and Means Committee for a solid year. At the start of the new session in 1971, it was honored with the designation of H. B. (House Bill) 1. Months later the House passed the reform bill. At this writing it is in the Senate where a similar process of foot-dragging is going on.

Later in 1971, Mr. Nixon proposed a bold plan to share federal revenues with the state and local governments to enable them to cope more effectively with their problems. Mr. Mills, perhaps rightly, for the plan poses serious problems, was personally opposed. Nevertheless, he agreed to hold hearings in recognition of the fact that a real need to finance state and local governments existed. The President's measure need not have been enacted as recommended. Mr. Mills's committee had ample opportunity to draft an alternate means of solving the problem. But absolutely nothing has happened. This is the tragedy of Congress. Nothing very much happens.

Hundreds of similar examples, all of recent origin, could be cited. The nation suffers under a do-nothing Congress. Even when it accomplishes something it is often so watered down as to be only a half measure. Too little is done too late.

Why? There are two major reasons, only one of which something can be done about, if the problem is viewed realistically.

Congress is a collection of men and women with local, parochial interests. As such it has the merits of representing a cross section of the attitudes and special interests of Americans. But when Congress tries to form a majority to accomplish something for the national good or to benefit a majority of the people, futility often results. Rural voters have little interest in urban problems and vice versa. Labor interests are often exactly the opposite of those of corporations. To try to weld some sort of majority is an exercise in exasperation.

One way to cope with the problem would be to adopt some kind of system such as the British have. The national Democratic and Republican parties would have to be reorganized so that financial and policy controls were instituted from a national office.

Also, the British do not have residency requirements. In the United States, a person must reside in the state or district in which he stands for election. Not so in Britain. The prime minister and other important government officials are frequently assigned safe districts, so they do not have to worry about being elected. Such a system has the advantage of making members of the British Parliament more national and less parochial in their interest. [2]

Short of these changes, some way will have to be found in America to force national party discipline on individual members of the party in Congress. On important measures at least, ways would have to be found to force recalcitrant senators and representatives to follow the policies the national leadership of the party has selected.

There is a possibility of doing this, which introduces the second reason for Congress's ineffectiveness — its own rules for conducting its business.

At the beginning of each session of Congress, members of the respective parties assemble in caucus and elect their leadership. These are the members of both parties who are held in the greatest respect and have the most influence. They are to lead and speak for the party in Congress. Later, the two houses assemble and elect the officers and leaders of their legislative branches. They are always the men chosen in the caucuses, for the majority party always outvotes the minority party.

The leadership positions vary between the two houses. In the House, the leading member of the majority is elected Speaker of the House. He presides at legislative sessions and stands third in line for the presidency; that is, he will become president in event of the deaths of the president and vice president. Beneath him are a majority leader and assorted whips. The minority party elects a minority leader and whips. The role of the whips is to make certain that members of the political party vote as the party leadership wishes, itself often an act of exaggerated futility. At this writing the Speaker is Democrat Carl Albert of McAlester, Oklahoma. He was 62 when elected in 1970. The majority leader is Hale Boggs of Louisiana. The minority leader is Republican Gerald Ford of Michigan.

In the Senate, the vice president, under the Constitution, presides, but as a practical matter the gavel is rotated among various senators. The senior member of the majority party is elected "President Pro Tempore," a rather honorary position meaning that he presides in the absence of the vice president. The principal leader is the majority leader, at this writing Democrat Mike Mansfield of Montana. Under him is a whip, now Robert C. Byrd of West Virginia. The minority leader in the Senate is Republican Hugh Scott of Pennsylvania.

These men have tremendous notoriety. They are widely interviewed on television and in the press. They frequently voice the opinions of their political parties, and their opinions on national issues are always valued and respected. But as a practical matter, their power is limited under congressional rules. Nevertheless, strong leaders can play most important roles. In recent times the strong leaders were Speaker Sam Rayburn and Senate majority leader Lyndon Johnson, both of Texas. Their influence stemmed largely from the power of their personalities and their ability to persuade their colleagues to do as they wished. There is nothing inherent in the power of either office to insure that a lesser or more distinterested man would have as much influence. Indeed, their successors have not.

It did not use to be so. Prior to 1911, the Speaker of the House was a virtual autocrat. As chairman of the Rules Committee he determined which bills came to the floor for debate and vote—or if they came to the floor. He assigned bills to the various committees. He appointed the chairmen of the committees and assigned their memberships. His was incredible personal power. He alone decided what Congress did and how.

In 1911, the House revolted against Speaker Joe Cannon of Illinois. Rules were changed so that the Speaker was no longer an automatic member of the Rules Committee. With that he lost his control over the order of business in the House. No longer could be appoint committee chairmen. Something similar happened in the Senate.

Today the powerful men in the Senate and the House

form an oligarchy of chairmen of standing committees, 21 in the House, 16 in the Senate.

There are those who feel Congress lost something when the elected leadership of the two houses were shorn of their power. Surely the autocratic ways of Speaker Cannon and his predecessors were bad, but today the leadership of the Senate and the House lack any sort of formal control over the committee chairmen and have a most difficult time leading their party activities in Congress.

The committee chairmen run Congress. A description of the power of these men was given by George Galloway in his book *The Legislative Process in Congress:*

> Just as the standing committees control legislative action, so the chairmen are masters of their committees. Selected on the basis of seniority, locally elected and locally responsible, these "lord-proprietors" hold key positions in the power structure of Congress. They arrange the agenda of the committees, appoint the subcommittees and refer bills to them. They decide what pending measures shall be considered and when, call committee meetings, and decide whether or not to hold hearings and when. They approve lists of scheduled witnesses, select their staffs, and authorize staff studies and preside at committee hearings. They handle reported bills on the floor and participate as principal managers in conference committees (between the House and Senate). They are in a position to expedite measures they favor and to retard or pigeonhole those they dislike. Strong chairmen can often induce in executive sessions the kind of committee actions that they desire. In the House of Representatives, where debate is limited, the chairman in charge of a bill allots time to whomever

he pleases during debate on the floor; he also has the right to open and close the debate on bills reported by his committee; and he may move the previous question whenever he thinks best. In short, committee chairmen exercise crucial powers over the legislative process.[3]

The chairman also appoints the chairmen of subcommittees which have exclusive control over areas of legislation. When the House Agricultural Subcommittee on Forests, for example, turns out a piece of legislation dealing with the lumber industry, the full Agricultural Committee does little more than re-arrange a few commas. The subcommittee is an independent fiefdom responsible only to the chairman of the full committee.

The committee chairmen, holding nearly exclusive power over their special areas of legislation, arrive at their positions of power through seniority. Every senator or representative is named to at least one committee. When first elected, all hope to be named to a powerful committee, such as Appropriations, Rules, Armed Forces, Banking and Currency, Judiciary, Ways and Means. Then, simply by being elected time after time, they become chairmen of powerful subcommittees or even full committees.

This means that committee chairmen almost invariably come from safe districts where they can be re-elected to repeated terms. In a Democratically controlled Congress, which the nation has had except for two years since 1933, committee chairmen tend to be overwhelmingly from the South and West. Of the sixteen committee chairmen of the Senate in 1970 – 71, ten were from Southern or Border states, five from Western states and one from the East. None was from the Midwest. In the House in the same Congress, eleven of the twenty-one committee chairmen were from Southern or Border states, three from the West, four from the Midwest, and three from the East. Among the ranking Republican members of committees, who would become chairmen in the event their party controlled Congress, the preponderance came from Maine, Vermont, New Hampshire, and the Plains states.

It is more than a little significant that the populous industrial states, with the exception of Texas, can boast few committee chairmen. California, New York, Pennsylvania, Illinois, Ohio, Michigan, and such states are highly deficient in committee chairmen. It is difficult to say why these states so frequently change senators and representatives. Perhaps their voting patterns are in a state of flux because of the mobility of the population. Whatever the reason, the preponderance of the powerful men in Congress come from rural areas. Power in Congress does not lie with those who represent populous urban industrial districts and states.

In part this is the fault of Congress. It failed for many decades to redistrict itself or to force the states to re-arrange congressional districts. Not very many years ago, Michigan had one congressman representing 802,000 people, another representing 117,000; Maryland had one for 711,000 people, another for 243,000; Colorado one for 653,000, another for 195,000; Ohio one for 724,000, another for 235,000. Some states had districts more than twice the size of the smallest and in five states the largest districts were three times the size of the smallest.

The effect was to give heavy representation to rural

areas, less to urban. The Supreme Court changed this by ruling that representatives must come from districts of approximately equal size. The effect was to make the House more responsive to the needs and wishes of urban, suburban, and populous districts.

But the Senate remains tied to rural interests. Under the Constitution, every state, regardless of population, must have two senators. This means that five states—Alaska, Delaware, Nevada, Vermont, and Wyoming—have two senators and only one representative. Another ten states—Hawaii, Idaho, Maine, Montana, New Hampshire, New Mexico, North Dakota, Rhode Island, South Dakota, and Utah—have an equal number of senators and representatives. The fifteen smallest states have an aggregate population of about ten million. approximately equal to that of Illinois. Yet, these ten million people have thirty senators, while Illinois has two. The ten largest states have a total population of roughly one hundred million, about half the total population of the United States, yet they are represented by only twenty senators.

The Founding Fathers intended this. It was the "Great Compromise" of the Constitutional Convention. But the result today, with the Senate controlled by senators from predominantly rural, farming, sparsely populated states, can be seen in the slums, urban decay, rotting housing, traffic jams, and polluted air of the nation's cities.

The senators from rural, farming, or sparsely populated states are interested in the welfare of the nation as much as the next person, perhaps more so, but it is simply not very politically expedient for them to vote for legislation that would tax their constituents to benefit the residents of large cities. Too, their attitudes are colored by their rural upbringing. They are simply less acquainted with the helplessness of the urban dweller.

Through the committee system, Congress divided itself into a collection of special-interest groups. All members of the House Agricultural Committee come from farming districts. There are no representatives of urban consumers. The committee further divides itself into subcommittees responsible for specific commodities such as cotton, tobacco, wheat, lumber. Members of these subcommittees represent, not the American people or even the people of their district, but these particular commodities. At election time, a member from a cotton-growing district is able to cite what he has done or tried to do for the cotton-growing business. Campaign contributions flow. Similar statements can be made by representatives of the corn belt, wheat belt, or lumber districts. They are virtually undefeatable and, because of seniority plus expertise, cannot easily be dislodged from their subcommittee or committee bailiwicks.

However, time marches on. The Supreme Court ruled and the House of Representatives was redistricted. Reflecting the nation's population patterns, the House came to be dominated by representatives from urban and suburban areas. Their main interests reflect the consumer, not the producer, of agricultural products.

What happens? A bill is reported out of the Agricultural Committee. It is drastically altered or defeated on the floor. The result is stalemate. Nothing happens to benefit anyone. There is a handy solution to the problem. The Agricultural Committee ought to concern itself with the interests of the urban consumer. It should report out bills dealing with hunger in America, such as food distribution programs; and dealing with school lunch programs, and with honest advertising of food products. A compromise could be reached. I'll vote for a food stamp plan if you vote a subsidy for cotton or wheat farmers. But the committee leaders, bound to parochial interests, do nothing. It is politically more effective for them to represent their special interests, accomplishing little, than to enact legislation which is of no interest to their districts, and might be unpopular there.

The House Education and Labor Committee is made up solely of members who represent those groups. The Labor portion of the committee is made up entirely of people highly sympathetic to labor.

Worse, much of the House represents nothing. Of its twenty-one committees, only ten have very much to do. For practical purposes its committees on the District of Columbia, Foreign Affairs, Government Operations, House Administration, Interior and Insular Affairs, Internal Security, Merchant Marine and Fisheries, Science and Astronautics, Standards of Official Conduct, and Veterans' Affairs have little or nothing to do. If they encounter a major bill once every ten years, it is an event. The Senate is better off, but at least half a dozen of its committees are moribund.

Then there is the extraordinary power of the House and Senate Appropriations Committees. All spending legislation originates there. Congress might pass, for example, a measure to appropriate funds for urban housing. But the amount spent is a separate measure originating in the Appropriations Committees. It is possible, indeed common, for the Appropriations Committees to emasculate the spending bills by approving only a very small amount. The Appropriations Committees, being so powerful, are composed of senior members who overwhelmingly represent Southern, Western, and rural states and districts.

The House Appropriations subcommittees, which have life and death control over specific areas of appropriations — agriculture, defense, District of Columbia, foreign operations, housing and urban development, interior, legislative, military construction, Treasury, Post Office, and executive offices — all have chairmen from Southern and border states. Only labor, health, education and welfare, which is one subcommittee; public works, transportation, and a subcommittee handling money for the State, Justice, Commerce, and Judiciary Departments have chairmen from the East, Midwest, or California. In the Senate, the situation is not much different.

The effect is to give rural, conservative interests two chances to block legislation for social purposes: first when the bill comes up for vote; then when money is spent. The situation can be reformed if Congress would amend its rules to return to the former system in which appropriation bills originated in the committees that fostered the legislation.

Clearly, Congress is badly in need of reorganization. This has been recognized for decades. Its own members have said so. Former Senator Joseph Clark of Pennsylvania has said Congress suffers from a "tyranny of the minorities."[4] A small group in the House, or one man in the Senate through a filibuster, can derail any action by Congress. The political parties have little control over their members in Congress. Congress practices government by coalition, trying desperately to find a majority to pass anything. Worse, even when there is a clear majority in favor of a proposal or a majority at least willing to vote on a measure, it is next to impossible to get the bill out of a committee on to the floor for a vote.

There is disagreement about how Congress ought to reorganize itself, but agreement that something must be done.

It badly needs new committee organization which more correctly represents the concerns of the people. If it can be argued that the shipping and fishery industries are worthy of a separate committee, so too can it be argued that there ought to be committees representing minority groups, environmentalists, the elderly, young people, health, suburban and urban residents, consumers.

Perhaps more important than the need for new committees is a committee structure that is national in scope. A committee structure in which only labor is on labor, business on commerce, farmers on agricultural committees is straight out of the nineteenth century. Clearly our national interests dictate a variety of opinions on these key committees.

There is nothing inherently evil in the seniority system. Those critics who talk of the doddering, senile old men holding power over legislation ignore the virtues of seniority. Youth commits as many sins as age. Many of the committee chairmen are experienced, extremely able, and notably progressive. Representative Emanuel Celler of New York, one of the oldest men in Congress, is a notable liberal as chairman of the House Judiciary

Committee. Nor does region make the man. Representative Wright Patman of Texas, chairman of the Currency and Banking Committee, is known for his pronounced progressive views.

If seniority were abolished and committee chairmen were chosen by a vote of party members in caucus, it would throw open the organization of Congress to the most unseemly sort of politicking, backbiting, and furore. Even greater stalemate would likely result.

Senator Clark has suggested two solutions to the problem. He would have the party caucus in Congress remove from a committee any member, including its chairman, who did not support the party's presidential nominee in the previous election. He would also have members and the chairman take a pledge to support the party's platform. Failure to do so would be grounds for removal.

Second, he would have the members of a committee elect their chairman by secret ballot. He believes that in nine out of ten cases the senior member would be chosen, but in those occasional cases where the chairman is autocratic and out of step with his own committee there would be the possibility of ousting him. Such a system, Senator Clark believes, would make the chairmen more responsive to the members of their own committees.

Many other rules need to be changed, but two are paramount. In both the House and the Senate, the Rules Committees have tremendous power, for they determine if and when a bill will be submitted to the floor for debate. A bill may be reported out by a committee, then be bottled up in the Rules Committee, which wastes time holding another set of hearings. The issue simply never comes to a vote. Clearly, in the House the procedural problems of the order of business could be easily solved in a short conference between the Speaker, majority leader, and minority leader. Why the Rules Committee needs to exist at all, other than as a fiefdom for senior representatives, is hard to figure.

Perhaps the most commonly known and denounced of the congressional rules is Senate Rule XXII. From it comes the famous filibuster. Any senator or group of senators may take the floor and talk as long as he wants to, relinquishing the floor only to whomever he wishes. Thus, a group of senators can prevent a vote by talking. Such filibusters have frequently stopped all consideration of a bill, indeed all Senate business, for days, weeks, and months. Historically, a two-thirds vote by the full membership of the Senate was needed to end the filibuster or achieve cloture. Some years ago, after prolonged debate, the Senate made a slight change in the rule to permit cloture by two-thirds of the members present. This made it easier to end filibusters, but they remain a fixture in the Senate.

Defenders of Rule XXII maintain that it protects minority rights, preventing the majority from submerging the interests of a minority. Congress, indeed the entire American government, has worked on the principle that no minority could be outvoted unless it agreed. A high degree of unanimity among the extremely divergent interests in Congress is necessary to pass anything. This is an unwritten rule, as is its exception. In the event of a national emergency, the members of a minority must surrender their special interests to the good of the nation.

For a long time the only way to get a bill of national importance through Congress has been for the president to declare an emergency or a temporary emergency. This has given rise to the trend to crisis actions. A series of presidents, trying desperately to get Congress to do something, have sometimes exaggerated threats to the national security, such as a Russian menace, a build-up of Russian weapons, a Communist takeover in Vietnam or some other land. Only in the crisis can Congress act quickly.

Congress needs to reorganize itself to permit a majority to rule. There are ample protections for the minority in the United States. The Constitution and the Bill of Rights spell out individual freedoms of Americans. The court system has a creditable record of protecting the civil liberties of minorities. The political parties are an amalgamation of minority opinions. There simply is little need for an additional barrier to majority rule in the United States Congress. Debate there should be. Compromise is inevitable. But when a majority consensus has been formed, Congress should find the way to act and quickly.

Perhaps the most pathetic effect of the ineptitude of Congress has been its giveaway of its powers. Unable to agree on nearly everything, it has for decades grabbed at a handy compromise. It gave the decision-making power to the president or some independent federal agency. This has given rise to the corporate state and to most undemocratic procedures.

9

The Presidency—
How It Grew

THE GREATEST CHANGE in the American form of government since the Constitution was written has been in the growth of the power of the presidency. The Founding Fathers had wanted a strong president, but that probably meant he was not to be weak. They greatly feared the tyranny of a monarchy. Today the United States does not have either a monarchy or tyranny, but the president is the most powerful single individual in the world.

The president's powers are those granted under the Constitution. They are easily enumerated. He is commander in chief of the armed forces; he may require the written opinion of any officer in the executive departments; he has the right to pardon offenders; he can make treaties with foreign governments, provided two-thirds of the senators assembled agree; he names ambassadors,

139

judges of the Supreme Court and other federal officers, again with the advice and consent of the Senate; he appoints lesser officers which Congress shall decree; he gives Congress information on the State of the Union; he recommends legislation to Congress; he may on extraordinary occasions call Congress into session or adjourn it; he is empowered to faithfully execute the laws; and he has the power to veto all acts of Congress, but the veto may be overturned by a two-thirds majority of the legislators.

That's all. It is difficult to conceive of how the modern presidency grew to such awesome power from such a paltry list of duties and powers. But it did.

It is doubtful if a full list of presidential powers and prerogatives has ever been compiled. Simply the major ones are impressive enough.

He personally commands a military force of 3.5 million men and women stationed in thousands of military bases around the world. These forces are equipped with awesome weaponry so that a single plane or rocket can unleash more destructive fire power than was used in all of mankind's previous wars put together.

He can engage the nation in military conflict without seeking, let alone receiving, the permission of Congress. Seven times since 1940, American presidents have engaged American troops in actions that could have or did lead to casualties. These actions were taken solely on presidential initiative. The list of seven does not count at least another dozen times in which presidents made minor commitments of American forces, or threatened to, or almost did.

He has been given or has assumed the power to make executive agreements with foreign governments. These commit the United States to other countries; yet only a handful of them were ever negotiated as treaties requiring Senate approval. In short, as a world leader, he has virtually sole authority for the nation's foreign affairs.

He supervises the preparation of the national budget, which now runs in excess of $200 billion a year. At a minimum, one of every ten dollars spent in the United States comes from the federal treasury. This gives the federal government an immense, yet highly personal impact on the national economy and every citizen.

He administers thousands of laws and is in charge of nearly three million federal employees, not counting members of the armed forces.

Through the executive branch he is able, if he wishes, to influence the regulation of business, labor, education, broadcasting, housing, poverty, health, conservation, and just about every other type of activity in the United States.

He can commandeer television, call in press reporters, address Congress virtually at will to explain his action or inaction, present the facts he wishes presented, keep secret those he does not want known, thus pleading a special case to the American people in defense of his conduct.

Kings have wished for as much power.

How did the president achieve it? His power just happened, inexorably, as a product of the weakness of Congress and state government, various crises, and the strengths of the men who have sat in the White House.

The office itself contributed to the president's power. He is the only man elected by all the people. The vice president is similarly elected, but by tradition he is selected by the president and his office is virtually powerless.

In the beginning the states were all-powerful, but America is a long way from that. Figures could be cited showing the increase in state and local employment, revenues, and expenditures. But these increases are largely for governmental services which can only be or are best performed at the local level. State and local governments employ teachers, policemen, firemen, collectors of garbage, transit workers, and many more. These activities and the expenditures for them are important. But the momentous decisions concerning foreign affairs, national defense, aid for health, education and housing, poverty control, anti-pollution measures, and hundreds of other matters of national and individual concern are made in Washington.

It didn't have to be so, but the states in large measure relinquished paramountcy over the lives of their citizens through decades of mal-apportionment. Rurally dominated do-nothing state legislatures ignored in large measure the problems of urban and suburban dwellers, who increasingly came to form the largest portion of the population. Seventy percent of Americans live in or near cities of 50,000 population or more. The urbanites came to look for aid to the only place they effectively could, the national government.

State and local governments also became increasingly impoverished. In 1913, the Constitution was amended to permit Congress to enact the federal income tax. It quickly came to be the largest money raiser in the country, far outdistancing state sales, local property, and various nuisance taxes (such as those on gasoline, tobacco, liquor, amusement). The impoverishment and often near-bankruptcy of state and city governments is a trend which is merely accelerating. Citizens came to look to Uncle Sam who had not only power, but money.

When the people, especially urban residents, labor, and members of minority groups, looked to Uncle Sam for aid they ran into the stone wall known as Congress. The ineptness of the national legislature, already described, led Americans to look to the one man elected by all the people who could offer the needed aid, the president. He was expected to lead the nation, suggest to Congress those laws which ought to be passed, and develop programs to aid various groups of citizens. Not parochially elected, he was expected to represent all the people and do what was best for them. Congress only assisted in this. Today Congress is largely unable to act until the president sends down *his* program. Few important measures originate in Congress. Moreover, Congress has given the president vast automatic powers over all phases of American economic and social life, as well as military and foreign affairs. Congress hardly needs to be consulted, except as a formality.

The Great Depression of the 1930s gave a tremendous boost to presidential power. It was a national economic cataclysm. A quarter of the work force was unemployed and those who had jobs worked for as little as five and ten cents an hour. In 1932, the people, rejecting Communism and Socialism, elected Franklin D. Roosevelt because he promised to remember the "forgotten man." He began an unprecedented program — aided by a Congress which was reacting to an emergency — which remade the economy into a form of state-controlled capitalism. The effects, too numerous to detail here, included a vast increase in the size of the executive branch. Nearly every form of public activity was regulated. Payments were made from the treasury to the poor, the unemployed, and the elderly. Money was appropriated for public works to create jobs. The government began to operate businesses. A vast spectrum of government activity and an immense bureaucracy to administer it — all at least nominally under the direction of the President — was spawned.

Then came World War II in 1941. The United States was thrust into, then increasingly thereafter assumed, the role of international interventionist. As the most powerful nation on earth, America came to the aid of other nations and interfered to a greater or lesser extent in their affairs. Fearing the imperialism of international Communism, we took on the role of world policeman. A large standing military force became necessary. Conflict and threatened conflict became constant. Crisis piled upon crisis.

Who was to act in such situations? Hardly the states. The Constitution forbade it. Congress? It had and has great power in military and foreign affairs, but no legislative body can act decisively in an emergency, be it real or imagined. At best it can pass laws, but it cannot administer them. Only the president could act, using his powers as commander in chief, executor of foreign affairs, and administrator of the laws. The powers of the office grew. American voters elected each postwar president in the expectation that he alone would act to defend the nation and protect its interests.

There is one other ingredient to this mix of presidential power: the precedents set by the strong men who have sat in the White House through history. George Washington refused to allow Congress to see messages from ambassadors and dispatched troops to quell the Whiskey Rebellion in Pennsylvania. He made the presidency independent of Congress or the states. He set a tone of dignity, impartiality, and legality under the Constitution which his successors have been hard-pressed to follow. Andrew Jackson, kept once from the White House by the House of Representatives, ignored Congress or made it come to heel, defied the Supreme Court and forced South Carolina to obey a federal law.

Abraham Lincoln, faced with open rebellion by the Confederacy, took whatever action he felt was necessary to preserve the Union and left Congress to come along later and ratify what he had done. Theodore Roosevelt developed the "stewardship theory" that it was the duty of the president to do all he possibly could for the people, limited only by specific prohibitions in the Constitution. Woodrow Wilson enlarged the presidency through use of personal persuasiveness. He resumed the practice of making direct addresses to Congress and innovated the presidential press conference. In World War I he took just as bold actions as Lincoln had, but he found ways to induce Congress to give him the needed authority.

Each of these strong presidents was followed by one or more less dynamic men, but even the weakest did not hesitate in an emergency to fall back upon the precedents set by former presidents. More, the presidency, as an office, came to be revered, even sanctified. The occupant took on, if not infallibility, at least supremacy.

Every president since Franklin Roosevelt has been a strong president. He cannot help but be. The duties of his office, the tasks assigned to him, the role he plays in national life all insure that the most timid and reluctant of men will be dynamic. An illustration of this point is recently at hand. Richard Nixon cannot be described as timid or reluctant, yet he had long avowed a personal philosophy of government which abhorred undue government interference in economic affairs. Repeatedly, he had made known his dislike for wage and price controls, unbalanced budgets, high government spending, and excessive use of presidential appeals to industry and labor to hold down wages and prices. Early in his administration, he developed a "game plan" to lower prices and increase productivity and employment without recourse to government intervention.

Then, in the summer of 1971, faced with public dissatisfaction over the worsening economic conditions, he did a complete turnabout. He announced a program of wage and price controls, even freezing both wages and prices for ninety days. Tax cuts were requested. Federal spending was reduced. The nation stopped payment of gold to other countries and imposed a 10 percent tax on imports. His philosophy of a lifetime notwithstanding, the President was forced to act. He set forth the most drastic economic program by government since the New Deal in the 1930s.

This illustration also serves another point. The modern president is the most responsive, or perhaps the least unresponsive, of any institution in any level of government in the United States. The charge of unresponsiveness cannot really be made in fairness against recent presidents.

The charge that can be made is that presidents have perhaps done too much and, more pertinently, that it is difficult to find out what they are doing.

On December 21, 1970, a blue ribbon subcommittee of the Senate Foreign Relations Committee released a report on United States commitments to other nations.[1] The subcommittee was chaired by Democratic Senator Stuart Symington of Missouri, a former secretary of the air force. The subcommittee made exhaustive inquiries both at home and abroad. Dozens of witnesses were questioned. This was the first thorough study of American commitments abroad in decades. The subcommittee's findings, covering the entire postwar period under both Democratic and Republican presidents, were shocking. A careful report on or analysis of these findings is beyond the scope of this book, but they may be briefly summarized here:[2]

The Symington subcommittee found that the United States was "firmly committed" to 43 nations by treaty and agreement and had some 375 "major" foreign military bases and 3,000 "minor" military installations around the world;

Many of these agreements were negotiated by a series of presidents without the concurrence of any other branch of government;

Many of the agreements were secret, and Congress,

let alone the people, was unaware of the extent to which the United States had been committed to aid foreign nations; [3]

American military forces were bound to those of other nations through joint military maneuvers and joint plans for defense of the other nation;

Other nations succeeded in committing American forces to possible future combat by permitting American bases to be developed in danger zones, an example being the insistence of the South Koreans that one American division remain on the border with North Korea so that an attack on the South would be an attack upon American forces;

Various presidents had so misstated the facts to the people or to Congress about American commitments abroad or their impact that a charge of duplicity could easily be (and was) leveled.

It became incredibly difficult, even impossible, for Congress, let alone the people, to find out what was going on. Actions of the members of the executive branch were labeled "top secret" or "secret," meaning the national security was involved. (This may, of course, be true in many instances; nevertheless the public was thereby prevented from knowing what had gone on.) Pertinent information on foreign affairs was refused to the congressional subcommittee. We became, in short, no longer an open, democratic society, but a closed, secret one. Combating Communism and maintaining a strong military deterrent to it became an end that seemed to justify nearly any means.

The Symington report set out chapter and verse of the growth of presidential power in foreign affairs. But the report was largely ignored. A few of its findings were reported in the press, but it failed to capture the public imagination. This was accomplished with the publication of the Pentagon Papers.

On June 14, 1971, the New York *Times* began publishing excerpts from and commentary about a history of the war in Vietnam which the Department of Defense (the Pentagon) had prepared some years before. Gray column after gray column was filled with words from the report. Almost twenty-four hours elapsed before the nation realized what the tens of thousands of words really said. Then the dam of public controversy broke.

To this day the full facts are not known, but the general consensus is that Robert A. McNamara, Secretary of Defense in the Kennedy and Johnson administrations, became increasingly disenchanted with the war in Vietnam. He ordered a study of how America became involved in the war. Thirty to forty authors were employed. After studying documents in the Pentagon, many of which were classified as "top secret," they wrote a massive history of the war. It ran to 2.5 million words (by comparison this book is only about 55,000), and over 7,000 pages. A small number of copies were printed and virtually all were labeled "top secret." Only a handful of people knew of its existence.

What happened then is a subject of dispute, court litigation, and perhaps misinformation. But the version most commonly given in the press—the nation may be years in discovering what really happened—is that a former government employee named Daniel Ellsberg, perhaps assisted by others, had photocopies made of most of the history. These he managed to get into the hands of first the New York *Times*, then the Washington *Post*, finally a number of other newspapers known to be critical of the war in Southeast Asia. The *Times*, which broke the story first, assigned a team of reporters to the story. They worked for months on the voluminous report.

The federal government viewed the documents as classified material which had been stolen and published without authorization. The Department of Justice obtained court injunctions to stop publication of the material in the *Times* and the *Post*. Attorneys for the newspapers ultimately carried the case to the United States Supreme Court where, by a 6-3 vote, they won the right to continue publication. The issue that went to the high court was freedom of the press versus the right of government to classify or conceal material of vital national interest. A succession of judges could find little in the Pentagon Papers that seemed vital to national security. The contents were simply embarrassing to former government officials. Freedom of the press won. The crucial legal point was that the government had no right to stop publication. The term for this is "prior restraint." After publication, the government had a right to prosecute if any laws were violated, but it could not censor prior to publication.

Sadly, the freedom of the press issue obscured what was important about the Pentagon Papers. They are excellent source material about how the nation went to war and the previously secret mechanism by which warmaking decisions are made, then "sold" to the Congress and the people.

It is possible to begin to put the Pentagon Papers into

perspective. As a history, they are terrible. They are so bad the word history cannot truly be applied to them. The study was written by a large number of people, almost none of whom have been identified. Their qualifications, their bias toward the war, and the information they possessed are totally unknown.

Moreover, the authors had access only to information in the Pentagon. They had no access to papers in the State Department and the White House, where much information was compiled and where many of the crucial decisions of the war were made. There are no interviews with pertinent individuals in the decision-making process, including Presidents Truman, Eisenhower, Kennedy, and Johnson. The report contains many memoranda suggesting possible actions in the war, but there is seldom any way to discover who saw the memos, if anyone did, and the effect they had on presidents and others who made decisions. Much of the papers contain "contingency plans"; that is, proposals for possible future actions in the event certain favorable or untoward events occurred. If those events do not occur, the plans are scrapped. Even if the events occur, an entirely new set of plans may be utilized.

The Pentagon Papers are laced with shortcomings. America desperately needs a full study to fill in what is missing so the original purpose of the report, how the nation went to war, can be fulfilled.

But, shortcomings or no, the Pentagon Papers are a revelation of the war-making process in the United States.[4] There is no need here to itemize the specific steps taken on the road to war. What is important are the general revelations of the decision-making process and how The System operates in the executive branch.

First, the road to war was inexorable. Presidents Eisenhower, Kennedy, and Johnson all traveled it. All were reluctant to engage in war, yet all were powerless to stop the forward march. They seemed pulled along by forces they could only partially control and could not halt. Some of these forces were opposition to Communist imperialism, a desire to halt the Communist expansion at any price including military force, a conviction that aggression must be halted early, that personal freedom is a common aspiration of all people and that they are or should be willing to endure any sacrifice for it. Finally, there was the belief in the invincibility of American armed might. Our national will, when exerted, could not be thwarted.

Second, all decisions involving foreign policy were the exclusive domain of the executive branch, particularly the president. Congress and the people should be consulted only for the purpose of ratification of what had already been decided.

Third, to achieve this ratification the essential facts were concealed, glossed over into a most favorable light, or even falsified, if necessary. Nothing is more shocking in the report than the evidence of duplicity. The American people were not told that in 1964 American military forces were secretly engaged in military operations against the North Vietnamese. During one of these operations, an amphibious raid on North Vietnamese offshore islands, American destroyers were attacked by North Vietnamese torpedo boats. The destroyers were in the general vicinity of the raiding forces. Even if the destroyers were not taking part in the raid, as America later contended, it is understandable that the North Vietnamese would think they were. Moreover, the destroyers were definitely on an "intelligence gathering" (a euphemism for spying) mission, according to the papers. These attacks on American ships (the raids, let alone American participation in their planning and execution, were not revealed) were used to persuade Congress to pass the Gulf of Tonkin Resolution. This authorized the president to "take all necessary measures" to "repel" an attack against American forces in Vietnam. The resolution became known as an "unofficial" declaration of war, although President Johnson insisted he had the powers to engage American forces even without the resolution.

The report indicates, although it does not prove, that in several instances false or certainly incomplete statements were made to the people about the war and plans for it. President Johnson said he knew of no plans to enlarge the war into North Vietnam in June 1964, when in fact plans for "retaliatory actions" had already been formulated. Mr. Johnson denied that the sending of additional American troops to Vietnam constituted a change in policy, whereas the Pentagon Papers indicate that the additional troops were seen as the start of American involvement in an Asian land war, one that would be long and require still more troops.

In September 1964, according to the report, a "general consensus" had been reached in the White House that North Vietnam would have to be bombed, yet at the time Mr. Johnson was campaigning for president as a candidate of "reason and restraint" against Barry Goldwater who recommended bombing the North. President Johnson insisted, in February 1965, that the United States wanted "no wider war" at a time one of his key assistants, McGeorge Bundy, was urging the President to adopt a program of "sustained reprisal" against North Vietnam to counter its attacks against South Vietnamese and American forces.

Fourth, as the plunge to war accelerated, a sort of self-perpetuating mechanism was created. Those advisers who counseled against the war or specific actions in it were shunted aside, ignored, or reduced to voices in the wilderness of war-making. The Central Intelligence Agency, for example, warned that bombing North Vietnam would be ineffective and would increase the determination of its citizens to fight on. This opinion, coming from such a powerful source, was nonetheless lost in the welter of opinion from military and other Pentagon advisers who wanted the bombing. What had been created was a high-speed tank without any brakes.

The Founding Fathers, as we have seen, created a government of checks and balances to prevent excessive use of power. This has created a situation throughout American history whereby it is difficult to form a majority or for a majority, when it exists, to act. In the Vietnam War an opposite situation prevailed. Like a struggling man in quicksand, the nation sank into its longest and most futile war unchecked, unbalanced. Clearly this is a great change in the American political system.

10

The Presidency and the Bureaucracy

THE PRESIDENT HAS vast powers. He is chief of state, greeting or visiting kings, prime ministers, and despots from other lands. He is chief executive, administering the national laws and programs; commander in chief; chief diplomat, determining foreign policies; chief legislator, recommending programs that Congress should enact; chief of his political party, organizing and leading it to remain in power; economic czar; inspirational leader educating the people to support programs for the nation's benefit; and finally world leader, influencing other nations toward peace or other goals.

All of this is a little much for one man. That fact reveals much about the powers and limitations of the presidency. All modern presidents have been hard-working—on the order of sixteen hours a day—dedicated, reasonably well organized. Yet even the most able of human beings is limited by time, attention span, and physical endurance. He can read only so much, see so many people, give attention to so many matters at once. Because of the nature of his tasks, he must limit himself to only the more important activities under his charge and delegate responsibility to others.

The presidency is not one but many men, many thousands of them. This fact reveals both the powers of the office and the limitations upon that power. It also reveals why the president is both carried along by the tide of events and why he is limited in what he accomplishes.

Who are these people who share presidential power? They are members of Congress, most particularly the powerful committee and subcommittee chairmen. They are members of his cabinet. These men are appointed by him and serve at his pleasure, but while in office they have direct legal authority over many matters.

The president also shares power with the heads of independent regulatory agencies, of which there is a large number. The list includes the Federal Reserve Board (members of which are appointed for fourteen-year terms), Federal Power Commission, Federal Trade Commission, Securities and Exchange Commission, Civil Aeronautics Board, Federal Communications Commission. These are independent agencies set up by Congress to supervise particular segments of the economy. A particular president may or may not appoint members of these commissions, since the terms do not always coincide with his, and he can influence their actions only with the greatest difficulty.

A large share of presidential power is shared with an

estimated 20,000 bureau chiefs. Some of these men, such as J. Edgar Hoover, director of the Federal Bureau of Investigation, serve at the pleasure of the president. But most do not. They are civil service employees who have risen to high rank through time on the job and/or ability and/or powerful political friends. They cannot be removed except by old age, ill health, or gross malfeasance in office, such as moral turpitude or the stealing of public funds.

A bureau chief has tremendous power over a small sphere of activity. Mr. Hoover has power over which federal criminal laws are to be enforced and with what vigor. He determines almost exclusively how his appropriation is to be spent and for what purpose. But the FBI is an obvious example. Consider a smaller bureau. There are men in the Department of Agriculture who determine what trees are to be planted or cut down and where. In the Department of Interior a man decides what fish and how many are to be grown in hatcheries and which lakes and streams are to be stocked. These men have great power over the lumber and sports fishing industries. It would be remarkable if a president could give half a minute's thought to these matters during his entire four or eight years in office.

Depending upon his style, the president shares his power with his personal staff. These are the men he sees most often. They determine his appointments, whom he sees, the mail and reports he reads, the information he has access to. They are delegated responsibility to deal with certain problems, be they at the cabinet or bureau level. More than any other president in history, Mr. Nixon has created a large White House staff which he trusts to act in his behalf. He is reported to have less direct dealings with cabinet officers, bureau chiefs, and regulatory agencies than any president in memory.

How is this vast federal establishment, numbering about three million men and women, organized? There is a textbook organization — cabinet level departments, divisions, bureaus, sections, with the White House, Congress, and independent agencies off to the side. Drawing such a table of organizations would surely be complex. Nor would it tell very much about where power lies in Washington.

Power in Washington is organized by vested interests. Virtually every industry, occupation, or attitude in the United States has representation in the federal establishment. Most often there are several layers of representation. Consider cotton farmers. The Agriculture Committees of the House and Senate include subcommittees made up solely of legislators elected from cotton-growing areas and interested in protecting and nurturing cotton production. The Department of Agriculture includes a bureau whose sole aim is to study cotton production and its problems and to take those actions necessary to improve the stability and prosperity of the industry.

In addition, cotton producers employ one or more lobbyists. These are individuals, perhaps former legislators or members of the Department of Agriculture, who are experts in the subject. They know all about cotton and its growth and marketing. They are expert on who has power over cotton problems in Washington. They know senators and representatives and key people in the Department of Agriculture and are intensely aware of their problems. The lobbyist is only helpful, providing important information to assist these people as they strive to benefit cotton producers.

Multiply this by any industry or enterprise you can think of — automobiles, aeronautics, textiles, shoes, all types of agriculture, the production of steel and other metals, packaging, all of them.

Nor is it just industry. Consider your teacher. He or she is personally represented on the education committees of both Houses of Congress. There is an Office of Education in the Department of Health, Education and Welfare. Its functions are further broken down into divisions, bureaus, and sections dealing with virtually every aspect of education. The organization to which your teacher belongs, or which claims to represent him or her, employs lobbyists who work diligently to improve education in general and the status of teachers in particular.

Congress has passed stringent laws requiring automobile manufacturers to install safety equipment in new cars and to control by some future date the polluting emissions from automobile engines. It was highly controversial before passage and was hard fought and is being fought hard still by the automobile industry. Yet this legislation was the product of the same system — congressional committees, bureau chiefs, and lobbyists for auto safety and anti-pollution laws.

There are exceptions, but in general it may be said that members of government, be they congressmen or bureaucrats, do not represent the people, but rather special or vested interests. Those who decry the corporate state speak only of those interests that represent industry or large corporations, while neglecting those also powerful groups representing education, the environment, housing, public welfare, civil rights, or peace.

And, of course, every time someone represents one vested interest, there is another person from an opposite vested interest to oppose him. Power in Washington is the playing off of one vested interest against another, an internal struggle for some kind of victory. If all this sounds familiar, it is. Washington is a mirror of the divisions that exist in the nation. It is also familiar because it is a restatement of the nation's difficulty in forming a majority and allowing it to act. It is another reflection of what Senator Clark called the "tyranny of the minorities."

As a theoretical exercise such a system might seem to encompass a large degree of democracy. And it does to a certain extent. Many minorities and special interests are represented in the federal government. There are spokesmen for a large number of opinions.

But closer examination reveals some problems. It is rather obvious that the automobile industry, say, as represented by General Motors, Ford, Chrysler, and American Motors, has a lot more money than the National Education Association. Whether or not they do it, the fact remains that the automobile industry has far more to offer in campaign contributions to would-be presidents, senators, and congressmen than do the nation's teachers. If that money is spent wisely by the automobile industry, it has far greater capacity to elect officials friendly to the automobile industry than teachers do to elect officials who will be concerned with educational problems.

It is also rather obvious that a large organization such

as the AFL-CIO has more political clout, based solely on membership, than do environmentalists. The NAACP (National Association for the Advancement of Colored People) can deliver a vote, at least in certain urban and Southern districts, which disorganized residents of substandard housing cannot. There is an inequality in the representation afforded various minority and special interest groups.

When a wealthy vested interest and/or a large numerical special interest combine with a basic national predilection, the result is sheer power. The leading example of this is the military-industrial complex. The desire for a strong national defense is so great it may almost be said that everyone is for it. The flag is waved and the need to protect mothers and children and the way of life cited. Defense is a strong predilection.

It also happens that national defense makes money for a small number of very large industrial corporations. In the eight years from 1962 through 1969 thirty corporations alone received $133 billion in defense contracts. More pertinent, the top five of them received over $50 billion and the top ten over $75 billion. The influence of such corporations was demonstrated in 1971. Congress took the unprecedented step of guaranteeing a $250 million bank loan for Lockheed Aircraft, the largest single defense contractor. Lockheed had gotten into financial trouble in building a civilian commercial airliner. It contended it was threatened with bankruptcy if the government did not guarantee the loan.

The large corporations are supported in the military-industrial complex by labor unions, whose members work in these industries. The livelihood of these workers is closely hinged to defense spending. Veteran and other patriotic groups identify themselves with a strong military posture.

The result of a national desire, immense corporate power, and widespread public support of labor is a vested interest of immense proportions. Whether or not such outlays for national defense are appropriate, it is quite clear that the number of large defense contractors and the men and women who work in them constitute a rather small minority of Americans. The preponderant majority receive no direct financial benefits from defense spending. Yet the combination, as reflected in Congress and the government bureaucracy, is overpowering. Half the budget goes for these purposes.

The minority rule of government takes on tyrannical qualities, too, because some extremely large minorities, indeed, possible majorities, are distinctly under-represented. The most obvious are urban dwellers. About seventy percent of Americans live in or near large cities. Yet these citizens are most ineffectually represented. Urban mayors trek to Washington to describe their financial plight and appeal for more funds, but not very much happens. There are a few organizations lobbying in Congress, such as the Urban Coalition and the National Municipal League, but these groups have never been able to gather the political power to force Congress even to create special committees representing urban and suburban residents.

Only in recent years have blacks begun to achieve political effectiveness. Indians have none at all. Public surface transportation, despite its status as a crying national need, has never managed to lobby as effectively for railroad passenger and bus service as the airline industry for its service. Conversely, the nation's agricultural industries are represented in Congress and in the bureaucracy to an extent those not engaged in such pursuits can only envy.

Perhaps the problem is that urban dwellers, for example, are so splintered that they are unable to form organizations as effective as those in agriculture. Probably more to the point is the mal-apportionment in Congress, already mentioned, which has long favored the rural resident and the farmer. Only recently have urban residents been adequately represented. They have not had time to develop their political muscle.

The government of the United States is a government by special interest. The one man who has the role of tying all this together is the president. He alone is elected by all the people. Blacks may not have voted for Richard Nixon, but when he takes his oath of office he in effect swears to represent them and to act for their welfare—or such is the common belief.

More practically stated, the president is the one man in the nation who can form a majority from all this variety and act in the nation's interests. Early in the book it was pointed out that there have been times in history when the majority did rule, when the nation found the way to act decisively for the national interest. Many times these actions were very late, but they did happen.

It takes no particular political acumen to see the situation in which this occurred. Mostly it happened in an emergency, such as wars or economic depressions. Fear and crisis have generated unity. Minorities surrendered their tyranny to the common welfare.

But there have been other times. In 1964, to give the most recent, Lyndon Johnson won the most sweeping majority in history and a Congress that supported his views. A host of what was labeled reform legislation was passed. Those who dislike the war in Vietnam may denounce Mr. Johnson for greatly escalating American involvement, but the success of his far-reaching domestic program cannot be denied.

It is a simple matter to say that what the nation needs to get moving or keep moving is to elect a president by a large majority and a Congress to support him. But that is whistling past the political graveyard. The American system does not always operate that way. Consider Dwight Eisenhower. He was elected by immense majorities in 1952 and the Republican party controlled both houses of Congress for the only time since 1933. Yet, nothing very much happened. Even General Eisenhower's most fervid admirers admit his eight years in the presidency were years of stagnancy. America's problems are worsened today because not very much was done about them during the Eisenhower administrations.

So what is the combination? Clearly something more than popularity and voter mandates for change are needed.

In his brilliant book, *Presidential Power: The Politics of Leadership*,[1] Professor Richard E. Neustadt sought to analyze the methods by which Presidents Truman and Eisenhower exerted leadership. It was a most influential book. President Kennedy carried it into the White House with him and Neustadt became one of his advisers. The book's examples are somewhat dated, as presidencies go, but his conclusions about presidential power seem as sound today as when written in 1960.

Neustadt saw the president as having power resources consisting of his acceptance among the people and his status in Washington. He could have the power of public opinion or the ability to get things done in Congress and in the bureaucracy, or he could have both.

President Truman lacked public support, particularly in the later stages of his term, yet he was widely respected in Washington for his ability to move Congress and the bureaucracy to do what he wanted. Dwight Eisenhower was greatly admired by the people (it is not too strong a word to say he was *revered*) yet he was so ineffective in Washington that at one point a congressional committee burst into laughter when he sent down a message expressing his determination to have a balanced budget.

But the illustrations go only so far. The simple fact is that a president, to be truly effective, must have the ability to influence public opinion and the skill to induce Congress and the bureaucracy to carry out his wishes. The consummate master of this, certainly in modern times and perhaps for all time, was Franklin D. Roosevelt. He could take to the air with a radio fireside chat and explain in simple, moving terms what he proposed to do. He won elections by large majorities. He knew how to present requests to Congress in such a way that Congress only rarely denied him. The bureaucrats, most of whom he had appointed, were in no position to thwart his wishes. No president since has been his equal. Kennedy was not in office long enough to make a clear determination. Upon his assassination, he seemed to be developing both bases of power. For a brief time after 1964, Lyndon Johnson had both, but squandered them on the war in Vietnam. It is extremely difficult to judge Richard Nixon while he is in office, but he seems deficient in both areas, particularly in his relations with Congress.

The magic ingredient that leads to forward movement in the American democracy is the president. He must be a man with the capacity to so inspire and lead the people that he has the obvious support of a clear-cut majority. Then he must have the persuasiveness to get Congress and its entrenched committee chairmen to do as he wishes.[2] Finally, he must be thoroughly aware of the attitudes of the bureaucracy, and have good enough assistants or be persuasive and threatening enough to get bureaucrats to do his bidding.

He must be *all* this. If he is deficient in any of the essential ingredients, his effectiveness will be lessened. The forces of division override the drive for unity. The majority gives way to the tyranny of the minorities.

It is an exaggeration to suggest that any president is powerless. When he wants a certain action performed and gives his attention to it, he can be denied only with difficulty. Encumbered with a hostile Democratic Congress, President Nixon asked for welfare reform legislation. He insisted and followed it up with an active program of support. Congress, not liking the program initially, has been forced to take action, however reluctantly or slowly.

A key element in Mr. Nixon's plan to end the war in Southeast Asia was to "Vietnamize it," that is, have South Vietnamese forces take over the burden of the fighting so American casualties would be reduced and GIs could be brought home. Because he knew that military commanders were cool to the idea, the President put Defense Secretary Melvin Laird in charge of the program. The best officers were put in command of Vietnamization and Laird demanded daily progress reports.

But a president, even using most effectively those to whom he delegates authority, cannot do all. In his presidency Mr. Nixon has given most of his attention to foreign affairs. But that attention has centered on American relations with Russia, China, Europe, and Southeast Asia. In the meantime, problems broke out elsewhere in lands left to underlings in the State and Defense Departments. India was considered a friend of the United States. Yet, upset by American support for its arch-enemy Pakistan, and what it considered lack of concern for its problems, India signed a friendship treaty with the Soviet Union. Japan, long a staunch ally, was stunned when it was not consulted or informed of Mr. Nixon's plans to visit Red China or to impose a 10 percent tax on imports into the United States. Situations have a habit of getting away from him, no matter how interested or energetic the President may be.

The Dr. Doolittle stories contain an animal called the "Pushmi-Pullyu." It goes both forward and backward, for it has a head in both directions. This is a reasonably accurate description of the relations all but the strongest presidents have with Congress and the bureaucracy. The Pentagon Papers clearly show that President Johnson was pushed toward full-scale war by the advice of military leaders, his own assistants, and leading members of the bureaucracy. Any president is a slave to the information he has. Even if he listens to the widest possible range of information, as did Franklin Roosevelt and John Kennedy, he is still influenced by those individuals in government in a position to be the most informed.

In foreign affairs that would be top State Department officials including ambassadors, military chiefs, the leader of the Central Intelligence Agency, the president's own staff of foreign experts. In domestic affairs, aside from his own staff, the president would listen to budget and treasury officials in economic affairs, members of the Commerce Department in business, officers of the Welfare Administration in social problems, and many others. If he receives misinformation, misguided opinions, or pays too much attention to what he wants most to hear, then the results are not exactly ideal.

Or, if he simply neglects a problem and leaves it to underlings, he is apt to be taken by surprise. As commander in chief, Mr. Nixon did not like or at least questioned the verdict of guilty and the life sentence imposed on Lt. William Calley who had been implicated in the massacre of South Vietnamese civilians at My Lai. Belatedly, the President stepped in and said he would make the final decision in the case. After a Soviet sailor jumped to an American Coast Guard cutter, Mr. Nixon was visibly upset when the Coast Guard permitted Soviet sailors to board the American vessel, beat and bind the defecting Lithuanian, and carry him back to Russia.

Nor can a president guarantee the results of what he wants done. Two consecutive Nixon appointments to the Supreme Court were denied by Congress. He wanted the nation to build a supersonic airplane, but it was denied. He wanted a start made on a new defense system against missile attacks and a $250 million loan guaranteed to Lockheed Aircraft. He won both by a single vote. The point is the president cannot guarantee any action from Congress, especially if it is dominated by the opposite party, and even if it isn't. And he cannot guarantee action by those under his nominal command in the bureaucracy. A bureau chief, particularly if he is a civil service employee, is a law unto himself. He was there before the president came and he will be there after he leaves. He may not be so discourteous as to say a direct "no" to a president, but he will engage in elaborate foot-dragging to delay doing what he does not want done. Most presidents don't even bother to ask a bureau chief to do what he cannot be convinced he wants to do.

This sort of charade seldom surfaces to public knowledge, but there have been enough examples to verify the existence of the problem. In the 1950s, President Truman nationalized the steel industry to prevent a strike during the Korean War. He later developed an elaborate plan to return the industry to private hands, while preventing a strike. He was undone by his Secretary of Commerce who disliked the whole scheme and did not want to be personally involved. The Secretary nominally agreed, but engaged in so much procrastination that the plan failed.

Earlier, Roosevelt's Secretary of the Interior foiled his chief by refusing to permit the exportation of helium to Germany, a prerogative authorized by Congress. The result was that Germany used explosive hydrogen to fill dirigibles. Following a disastrous explosion over New Jersey, a promising means of international transport was abandoned.

In 1970, during a civil war in Jordan, Richard Nixon wanted to make a dramatic show of American force. The Joint Chiefs of Staff were so negative about the plan and so unwilling to take the action the President wished, that the plan was scrapped.

The difficulties the president has in getting his wishes translated into actions have been plaintively expressed by a number of presidents. President Truman said, "They talk about the power of the president, how I can just push a button to get things done. Why, I spend most of my time kissing somebody's ass." Lyndon Johnson said, "Power? The only power I got is nuclear — and I can't use that."

To repeat for emphasis, any president is both pushed along by the information provided by his underlings and those he listens to and pulled back from what he wants to accomplish by the procrastination of these same people. This is particularly true in domestic affairs where congressional committee chairmen and bureau chiefs wield great power. But it is also true in foreign affairs, where the president's power is incorrectly presumed to be nearly autocratic.

11

The "Credibility Gap" and the "Corporate State"

MODERN PRESIDENTIAL POWER has provoked two issues which are much discussed by Americans. They are, as usually described, the "corporate state" and the "credibility gap." Both deserve special treatment here.

The serious charge is made that recent presidents have opened a credibility gap. In a word, they lie. This is a tough, tough charge that is, however, supported by considerable evidence.

The term was first used during the administration of Lyndon Johnson and has not abated under Richard Nixon. The basis for it is that these presidents made statements on various occasions which did not jibe with the facts as developed by reporters on the scene or supporting evidence as later made public to Congress and the people. The inference is that presidents have twisted the facts to suit their own purposes. Evidence to support the credibility gap is overwhelming and too voluminous to more than illustrate here.

In connection with Vietnam, Mr. Johnson and his key aides repeatedly issued statements predicting an American victory and an imminent enemy collapse which subsequent events proved to be grossly optimistic, to put the matter in most polite terms. In the Dominican Republic, Mr. Johnson justified the use of American troops to prevent "another Cuba," maintaining that the Caribbean nation was threatened with a Communist takeover. Reporters on the scene and subsequent events developed scant evidence of Communist infiltration. Mr. Johnson reported that the American ambassador to the Dominican Republic was cowering under a desk to dodge bullets while talking to the White House. Reporters could see no evidence of damage to the Embassy and no evidence that American civilians in the land were suffering.

Mr. Nixon dispatched South Vietnamese troops into Laos with American air support to attack North Vietnamese positions. The operation accomplished little and bore all the earmarks of a rout. Yet the White House insisted it was a notable victory. Under presidential auspices, a raid was long planned into North Vietnam to rescue Americans from a prisoner-of-war camp. With considerable daring and bravery, American troops conducted the raid, but found no prisoners to rescue in the alleged camp. The raid was nonetheless called a great victory and the commanders of the raid were personally decorated by President Nixon. In the background one White House aide told *Newsweek* magazine, "We are merchandising what remains one big flop."

Only a week or two before announcing his new economic program in 1971, Mr. Nixon was insisting that his previous economic program was a huge success and the economy would soon improve.

Because of the respect with which presidents and the presidency are held, the question is not usually put in such blunt terms as this, but do presidents lie? A plain question demands a plain answer. Yes, presidents do lie upon occasion and they frequently mislead through a combination of zeal, optimism, self-deception, and necessity.

There is a difference between a lie and a misstatement. To lie is to knowingly tell a falsehood; to make a misstatement is to state a falsehood believed to be true. The difference is in the motive of the teller. Since motives are an intensely private thing, it is difficult to tell a lie from a misstatement, although the effect may be the same.

There is at least one unmistakable case of presidential lying on record. In April 1961, President Kennedy used American military aircraft in support of an invasion of Cuba by exiles from that nation. When the Bay of Pigs invasion was defeated, Fidel Castro of Cuba proudly showed pictures of downed American planes to accuse the United States of invasion. The charge was denied by both the White House and by Adlai Stevenson, United States Ambassador to the United Nations. The plain fact is that everyone in the higher echelons of American government knew the Castro charge was true. They later admitted it.

There have been many other occasions when the rational mind dictates a charge of lying, but evidence is lacking of what went on in men's minds. Rationality dictates that President Johnson must have known that the American destroyers "attacked" by the North Vietnamese in the Gulf of Tonkin in 1964 didn't just happen to be passing by the neighborhood during an innocent passage on the high seas. Yet, he has not admitted what he knew, so his statements to the Congress and to the people must remain a misstatement.

The credibility gap is a relatively new and most serious development in the American political system. In truth, it is probable that such venerated national heroes as Washington, Jefferson, Jackson, and Lincoln engaged in it from time to time. But only a few historians ever became aware of it and even they did not discover it until much later. Today, newspapers and television networks are so militant about uncovering any public misstatements and so energetic in covering the news, that it is difficult to pull the wool over anyone's eyes for very long.

But such statements are dodging the issue. Americans pride themselves on being an open society. We brag of our "open door" policy toward the Orient early in this century when European nations were engaged in land and influence grabs. We like to think of those happy days when we were a "good neighbor" to Latin American nations. Woodrow Wilson spoke of "open covenants openly arrived at." Deeply ingrained in Americans is the belief that secrecy, evasion, misstatement, duplicity, and lies are major evils. Even liars believe one shouldn't lie. We would like to believe we prize morality higher than success.

Nevertheless, those who wish to understand the dissent and rebellion among the idealistic young in America need not look much beyond the abundant evidence of secrecy and deceit in America. The Central Intelligence Agency and our whole spy network is new in America and perhaps foreign to our nature. We simply are not very good at it. Militarism, though labeled "national defense," is foreign to what Americans were taught America was. Advertisers, expecially on television, clearly deceive about the usefulness and even the appearance of products — and candidates — in order to make money. An incredibly long list of misstatements can be compiled and labeled lies.

Though there is no documentary evidence for the statement, surely it is reasonable to believe that something valuable was lost in American political life with the rise in modern times of duplicity, misstatement, and lies. Some element of faith went out the window. Americans argued (and many still contend) that the exigencies of the Cold War against Communism and our role as a world power necessitated a bit of deceit. Indeed, in 1960, President Eisenhower was criticized for honestly admitting, after first lying about it, that the spy plane shot down by the Russians was ours and that we had been spying regularly on the Soviets in this fashion. It is apparently more difficult for his successors to make such admissions.

Those in their teens and twenties who decry the hypocrisy of The System may not be as far from their grandparents' thinking as they believe.

Of greater importance are these questions: How did it happen? How can an American president appear on television and speak a deliberate falsehood or so overstate the true facts that it is the equivalent? How did Americans, long dedicated to openness and truth, become involved in cloak-and-dagger spying, worldwide militarism, dishonesty, and self-deception?

Several answers might be given, but if we attempt to arrive at the basics of The System we must return to the nature of the democratic procedure and to the thesis of Professor Neustadt quoted in the last chapter.

An American president is the only man elected by a majority (and, as has been said, it is possible for him to be elected by a minority of the people). However small, that majority reflects majority thinking in terms of the man and what he hopes to accomplish. But under Neustadt's thesis, to rule he must find ways to influence and control both public opinion (his original majority or a new one) and the knowledgeable majority of Congress and the bureaucrats.

It is a horrendous task. The two audiences are different and he must attack the problem in different ways if he is to succeed. He attempts to marshal public opinion by taking to the airwaves and holding press conferences, by issuing public statements which are duly reported because they come from the president. He wishes to inspire confidence, so that he can win the support of public opinion in the hope that it will influence the members of Congress and the bureaucracy to do as he wishes.

Both necessity and human nature dictate that he present that information in the most favorable light. He may not lie, but he expresses optimism that the policies he espouses will work and cites the opinions of his most trusted advisers in support of his optimism. He hopes, and he believes what he is saying at the time he makes the statements. If later events do not work out according to his hopes and his beliefs, did he lie? Philosophers may ruminate over the problem, but the plain fact is that in America, being what it is, he was only trying, by the force of his personality, to fashion some kind of majority to get something done. If, by overstatement, by clever use of advertising techniques to play on audiences, he can fashion some kind of majority to support his plans, then he can go to Congress and the bureaucracy to state that the people want what he wants.

A succession of presidents have been driven along this route, trying desperately to place themselves and their policies in a most favorable light, never admitting failure, so they can form some sort of majority. In hindsight, it becomes rather pitiful, but at the time, hope being hope, it was a product of The System.

In dealing with Congress and the bureaucracy, the president has two choices. If he is a strong political leader, elected by a large mandate from a strong party which controls Congress as well as the presidency, he can use that power to overawe both the Congress and the bureaucracy. Congress is relatively easy, if the president is strong and popular. No senator, no representative can long stand up against a president who, as leader of the party, is in a position to deny patronage and funds to this individual. (An example is the 1970 election in

New York, where President Nixon supported a new-comer, Conservative James Buckley, rather than the liberal Republican incumbent, Charles Goodell.) If greater loyalty is given to the president, as chief of party, than to the legislator, the latter must surrender.

But if the president does not have this base of political power among the voters and the local party leaders, he is in trouble. If he was not elected by such a large majority as to claim a mandate, if he does not have sufficient influence among local party leaders, if he lacks the support of popular opinion, he faces difficult days. Or, if he is so lacking in knowledge of the bureaucracy and how it thinks and operates, if he does not realize where power in Washington lies, if he is not aware of how Washington's power structure will try to use him to its own ends rather than he use it to his ends, then the nation's course is deadlock and drift.

Into this mix must be added the Washington press corps. If the president and his staff cannot be helpful to columnists and reporters and commentators, providing them with an apparently unending succession of scoops, beats, private interviews, and late-breaking news, he runs the risk of their scorn, criticism, and unfavorable stories. The awful truth is that even if he does everything to woo the press, it may still turn against him, as a spoiled child turns against an indulgent parent.

A president has a couple of choices in this situation. One way (Franklin Roosevelt was a master at it) is to so charm and persuade bureaucrats, congressmen, and the press that they will do what he wants. It surely is an exhausting, time-consuming exercise, but it is one way to get things done. If he has offered a definite program to the people and is supported by a sizeable majority, he can appeal to public spirit to accomplish his will.

The second technique is to ignore the stumbling blocks in Congress, the bureaucracy, and the press. Of recent presidents, Richard Nixon is the master at this. He has surrounded himself with a large staff of assistants who are given great power over both the information he receives and over bureaucrats. To a large measure he has cut himself off from the rest of government. By holding few press conferences, he has isolated himself from the press. Such major decisions as the invasion of Cambodia and the planned visit to China were reached largely in the White House without prior consultation with any other informed group in the government. Their reaction may be fury, but there really isn't very much they can do about being ignored. Such a system has the advantage of enabling the president to accomplish a few things he really wants done, but makes it more difficult for him to control the large number of things the bureaucracy must do. Too, the process of government becomes much more secret.

It is not a defense of the credibility gap to state that it is to a large degree forced upon the president by the exigencies of military actions, spying, secret negotiations with other nations who do not have open societies, as well as the need for the president and the bureaucracy to do what he believes the majority wants done or what he thinks ought to be done for the good of the country. It may be argued that presidents could be more honest and open. But surely, in part, the sheer task of moving a government of special interests to do anything forces chief executives into misstatements and the position of putting essential facts in the most favorable light.

But even if such considerations are given the most that can be granted to them, many Americans are left with the impression that recent presidents have been less than candid. The credibility gap does exist. Some scholar should attempt a study of its origins and development. The beginnings are hard to figure, but surely in modern times the lie of Mr. Kennedy over the Bay of Pigs invasion of Cuba was extraordinarily disillusioning. Americans, who had always believed in presidential statements, began to question, which made things more difficult for each succeeding president.

Sooner or later men campaigning for the presidency will come to the realization that Americans admire honesty, appreciate the truth, are able to take bad news, and desire candor more than deception. Much of the criticism of The System is in pursuit of such goals.

Somehow criticism of the credibility gap has been equated with the corporate state, although the two are distinctly different problems. It is eminently possible to have a non-corporate state and a credibility gap at the same time or vice versa.

The term "corporate state" is the most commonly used. It was, for example, the title of a chapter in Charles Reich's *The Greening of America.* [1] Others use the words "power structure." Economist John Kenneth Galbraith called much the same phenomenon the "new industrial state" in a book by the same name. [2] With apologies to both men and to others who have written about essentially the same thing, it must be said that the problem is much older and was recognized by earlier scholars of considerably less popularity. Beginning in the mid-1950s, sociologist C. Wright Mills of Columbia University used the term the "power elite" to describe who has power in America and how they use it. At the time Mills, now deceased, was both applauded and criticized for his insight, and has been ever since.[3]

By whatever name, the basic issue is that the United States is undemocratic. The charge is that decisive power lies, not with the people, but with a small group which takes upon itself the task of acting in the name of the people. The inference is that such a "democratic" procedure does not differ to a notable degree from the "democratic" procedures of the Soviet Union or Communist China.

That, too, is a tough, tough charge and there is considerable evidence to support it. The corporate state makes the government unresponsive and gives the people little control over their affairs.

What is the corporate state? The inference is that government in the United States, principally the federal government, is controlled and run by men who have a vested interest in corporations, banks, law firms that represent them, or other symbols of wealth. Professor Mills, studying the Eisenhower administration in 1953, declared that fifty men composed the power structure. He listed the president, vice president, members of the cabinet, assistant secretaries of those departments, the military chiefs, and the heads of large independent agencies and bureaus. He found that only a quarter of these

men had any sort of political background; that is, that
they had been elected to any office, however minor. All
the rest were rich men, members of corporations, professional military officers, or members of law firms serving
corporations and the wealthy. Such groups as the poor,
the middle classes, university scholars were not represented.

There were serious faults with the Mills thesis. He
misunderstood where power lies in Washington. He
should have included the chairmen of powerful committees in Congress. He should have compiled a much larger list. In their domains, the heads of even small bureaus
wield great power. Indeed, in many instances, bureau
chiefs have reduced cabinet secretaries and their assistant secretaries to mere figureheads.

But these faults do not eliminate Mills's central thesis,
that the federal government is run by a relatively small
power elite which is a product of or in the service of
wealth.

Others have added to Mills's work. America is said to
be a corporate state because large companies, through
campaign contributions and other forms of financial influence, are able to dictate to politicians and control the
actions of the federal establisment. Modern campaigning
requires millions of dollars for a candidate in a large district. This money can be easily supplied by wealthy individuals and corporations, and these contributions can
insure that the candidate remains friendly. It is only natural for the officeholder to listen to the advice of those
who have supported him the most. Too, the contributors
have the interest of the nation at heart and are giving

what they think to be good advice. As Charles Wilson, a Secretary of Defense in the Eisenhower administration, said, "What's good for General Motors is good for the nation."

Wealth also influences members of the bureaucracy. Through a process of flattery, supplying of useful information, persuasion, and favors, lobbyists for the wealthy are able to have key bureau chiefs think and act for their benefit. Indeed, most of the bureaus were set up to serve the needs of various vested interests. Under such a system, it is inevitable that they would serve the groups they represent.

Evidence of the corporate state is more specific than these generalities. Large numbers of people leave government service to work for corporations. The television industry has a significant number of executives who formerly worked for the Federal Communications Commission, which regulates the industry. United States Attorneys and members of the anti-trust division of the Department of Justice are eagerly sought as corporate employees. Airlines grab employees of the Civil Aeronautics Board. A dozen other examples could be cited, but the most pronounced illustration is the employment of retired military officers by defense contractors. A general or an admiral is employed to call upon the members of the military who succeeded him in authority. The successor often owes his promotion to the retired officer, who now represents a defense contractor.

Corporations and government are intertwined. Government recruits its top appointees from corporations and corporations employ ex-government executives.

And all this activity is highly concentrated. Repeated studies have shown that a few hundred large corporations control half the nation's employment, production, and research. Government talent is recruited from a handful of corporations, which in turn hire talent from government sources.

This is an extremely serious condition for a democracy. A poor man cannot be elected to any office larger than congressman unless he accepts money from wealthy contributors and the influence that goes with it. Regulatory agencies of the government are more likely to represent rather than regulate the industries they are supposed to control. With certain large minorities, such as blacks, urban dwellers, environmentalists under-represented in Congress and the bureaucracy, while great power is accorded to industry and wealth and agriculture, a clearly undemocratic situation results. The charge that America is a corporate state may have become rhetoric with certain dissenters, but it is rooted in a large body of fact.

A search for solutions to the problem begins with the realization that there are many exceptions. Since its inception, the Securities and Exchange Commission has vigorously represented the small investor. It has not become an agent for the stock exchanges, stock brokerage firms, or large investors. It has scrupulously sought to make and keep the sale of stocks and bonds as honest and fair as possible. After many years of slavish bowing to the pharmaceutical industry, the Food and Drug Administration has in recent years begun to demand higher standards for new drugs, correct labeling of existing ones, and to challenge the continued sale of largely worthless nostrums. The Senate Foreign Relations Committee, after years of "yesing" presidents, has begun to investigate and question the nation's foreign policy. Its membership has been aggressive in seeking an end to the Vietnam War.

The problem with citing such examples of government agencies that work in the public interest is to decide what the public interest is. In a nation such as America there is wide disagreement over the definition. General Motors is as much a part of the United States as the Black Panthers. The Daughters of the American Revolution are as American as the Students for Democratic Action. What is the public interest? Industrial corporations have as much right to good government as labor organizations, although their goals may be different.

A handy solution would seem to be majority rule. That which is of greatest benefit to most of the people is what government should do. But there are instant problems. For one, most people do not know what they want or what is beneficial to them. Writer Walter Lippman is among those who have pointed out that many of the most vital issues of today are too complex to be understood by non-experts.[4] Such matters as the gold drain, balance of payments, financing the national debt, taxation, erection of low-cost housing, legal issues in pollution are of vital concern to most Americans, but understandable only to the most technically expert. Lippman has pointed out that one of the reasons why the Senate has ceased to be a forum for great debate is that the issues before it are now so complex that most senators don't know enough about them to discuss them.

Moreover, even when the issues are understandable or experts are employed to make them understandable, intelligent, reasonable, public-spirited men and women disagree about what should be done in the public's interest.

The need for expertise in complex matters is one reason why government tends to recruit its important men from corporations and why corporations tend to hire former government employees. If you were president and looking for an ideal man to head one of the cabinet-level departments, you would desire a man with such abilities as intelligence, patience, aggressiveness, administrative experience, expertise in the field, energy, self-lessness, self-discipline. These happen to be the qualities that lead to success in almost any endeavor. You would be most likely to find such a man among corporate executives, university professors, military leaders, and experienced government officials. It might be democratic to make a ditchdigger the Secretary of Labor, but it is unlikely that he would be very able in supervising such a large agency.

Furthermore, the men with expertise and administrative skill tend to be in demand and highly paid. It is perhaps inevitable that they be men of wealth. Making money is one of the easier occupations in America today. Almost anyone with desire and know-how can accomplish it. Too, Americans have long accepted men of means as leaders. Consider George Washington and the other Founding Fathers. We may admire the Jacksons, Lincolns, and Hoovers who were born in log cabins, but only if they later acquired wealth. Moreover, many of the most prominent and progressive men in government have been born to wealth, including the Roosevelts, the Kennedys, and the Rockefellers. The idea seems to be that if a man is independently rich, he can give himself entirely to public service and not be tempted by bribes.

But all this is begging the issue. Corporate influence in American government is too large and too insidious. The nation's premier problems of urban decay, equality for minority groups, pollution, surface transportation are principally those in which corporations have taken the least interest. Low-cost housing is a desperate American need, but it just doesn't make much money.

The untoward influence of large corporations in government can be reduced in two ways, aside from general revolution destroying the whole system. Since the United States is a government of vested interests, one way is to enlarge the representation of those speaking for large groups of people. Clearly, the poor, the urban, the black need to insist upon separate, special representation such as corporations enjoy. If there were a department of urban affairs, a pollution council, a larger poverty agency, they would be more representative of these groups and more vigorous in representing them in Congress and the Administration.

A second way would be for the cabinet departments and independent agencies to be more attuned to the *public* interest than the vested interest. Lip service aside, it has been a long time, if ever, since the Interstate Commerce Commission, the Federal Trade Commission, the Federal Communications Commission, the Department of Agriculture, and many other agencies considered themselves responsible for representing the public interest rather than those they are supposed to regulate. As evidence, one must only consider the low state of passenger train service in the United States, the plethora of clearly fraudulent advertising on television and radio, the high cost of food and fiber staples, while small farmers are driven to bankruptcy.

Clearly, there is another way. These long-established, largely moribund agencies could be revitalized to work for that which is of general benefit to the nation, rather than that which is of benefit to special interest groups.

A reorganization of the executive branch may be in order. One proposal, made in 1971 by a commission headed by businessman Roy Ash, would consolidate the independent agencies into half a dozen cabinet-level departments under an officer serving at the pleasure of the president. It would give the chief executive greater control over the vital activities of these agencies. As a result, the agencies could, it is hoped, be made more responsive to the public interest and to the programs of the president.

12

The Supreme Court

ONE OF THE most profound changes in the American political system from that designed by the Founders has been in the enlargement of the power of the judicial branch, especially the United States Supreme Court.

The nine justices of the high court, most definitely a minority of citizens, have today what amounts to a veto power over acts of Congress or state legislatures, over actions of the president or any other elected official, and decisions of any lower federal or state judge or jury. The fact that they do not often use this power does not abrogate the fact of its existence. Furthermore, the Supreme Court has the power to initiate programs and policies — that is, make law — of its own choosing and compel others to administer its programs.

The initial assumption of power was made by the

court in an opinion by Chief Justice John Marshall in 1803 in the case of *Marbury v. Madison*. It might be supposed that an opinion of such far-reaching importance would have been rendered in some case of classic proportions. But it was not. William Marbury was one of several "midnight appointments" made by President John Adams just prior to his leaving office on March 3, 1801. Marbury was appointed to a five-year term as justice of the peace in the District of Columbia. Inadvertently, Marbury's commission, signed and sealed, was not delivered to him, but was left on the desk of the Secretary of State when Adams's term expired. Thomas Jefferson, next in the White House, ordered his Secretary of State, James Madison, not to deliver the commission to Marbury, who, in turn, went to court to compel Madison to give him the job. In technical terms, but of importance to American history, Marbury sought a writ of mandamus, that is, an order from the court, under Section 13 of the Judiciary Act of 1789 (one of the first acts of the first Congress setting up the federal court system), that he be given his appointive post.

Chief Justice Marshall, speaking for the court, decided that Marbury had a right to the commission, that it was bestowed on him in a legal manner, that the refusal to deliver it to him was a "plain violation" of his rights. Marshall further ruled that Marbury was entitled to a court order by which his commission would be delivered to him.

Only one question remained, in Marshall's view. Did the Supreme Court have the power to issue the writ? Was Marbury in the right court? The Judiciary Act, duly passed by Congress, said Marbury was in the right court. Marshall ruled that the law violated the Constitution and was thereby null and void. In such picayune matters is history so often changed.

The legal question involved in the case is almost lost from view. Article II, Section 2, of the Constitution reads, in part: "In all cases affecting ambassadors, other public ministers and consuls, and those in which a State shall be party, the Supreme Court shall have original jurisdiction." Marshall did not see that the list included justices of the peace in the District of Columbia; therefore Marbury had no right to go directly to the Supreme Court and the law which entitled him to do so was wrong and unconstitutional. Marbury would have to go to a lower court and then appeal to a higher court if necessary.

Most of the Chief Justice's argument deals with the power of the Supreme Court to declare an Act of Congress in violation of the Constitution. His line of argument is worth following.

The Constitution, he pointed out, defined or limited the powers of its separate branches, such as Congress and the president, as well as the states. He maintained that the Constitution clearly intended that the limit on the powers of Congress not be exceeded. Also, the Constitution controls any legislative act "repugnant" to it, else Congress could pass any act it wanted to and the effect of this would be to amend the Constitution. Thus, instead of making amendment to the Constitution difficult, as the drafters intended (two-thirds majority of Congress and ratification by three-fourths of the states) the Constitution could be changed by a simple majority of Congress. Marshall argued:

> It is emphatically the province and duty of the judicial department to say what the law is. . . . If two laws conflict with each other, the courts must decide on the operation of each. So, if a law be in oppostion to the Constitution; if both the law and the Constitution apply to a particular case, so that the court must either decide that case conformably to the law, disregarding the Constitution, or conformably to the Constitution, disregarding the law, the court must determine which of these conflicting rules governs the case. This is of the very essence of judicial duty.[1]

For the courts to place a law above the Constitution would be to subvert the Constitution. It would greatly enhance the power of the legislature, when the Constitution sought to limit it. Without judicial review of legislative acts, the Constitution is reduced to "nothing," Marshall argued. He gave a number of examples of how Congress might subvert the Constitution, such as by enacting an Ex Post Facto law when it is expressly forbidden. Finally, he concluded that the courts were to decide the constitutionality of the law because judges take an oath of office to support the Constitution.

As was pointed out at the time, Marshall's argument was rather flimsy. Members of Congress, the president, and other officials also take an oath to support the Constitution. In the case of Congress, the people have recourse if members violate their oath to enact constitutional laws. The laws can be amended or rescinded by a subsequent congressional act. The members of Congress can be defeated at the polls and another Congress can undo what the former did. A president acting unconstitutionally can be defeated or become so unpopular as to be threatened with defeat. If corrupt, he can be impeached by Congress. The people simply have less recourse to the Supreme Court. Its members serve for life or until retirement. For practical purposes, there is no way to undo their decisions unless they wish to do so voluntarily.

For practical purposes. That is the key phrase. Actually, the Supreme Court's powers are derived from Congress and tradition. Congress could change the court by enlarging its membership or limiting the types of cases it can consider. Only a simple legislative act would be required. The Court has virtually no administrative staff. It is dependent upon the executive and legislative branches to carry out its edicts. Andrew Jackson refused to. Many other branches of the federal, state, and local governments contrive to ignore or thwart court orders. The high court may have ordered public schools racially desegregated in 1954, but in 1971 it was largely a nominal exercise, particularly in the North.

The power of the Supreme Court is the power of public opinion. It has been said that "no Supreme Court in American history has ever defied for long the sustained will of the dominant opinion in the nation."

Throughout its history, the court has swayed back and forth on most public issues, advancing and then retreating, occasionally coming out with a courageous defense of liberty or civil rights. It has in the main taken the side of the dominant opinion of the times.

Yet the Supreme Court remains extraordinarily re-

vered in America. Nominees to the court are carefully
reviewed by both the president and the Senate. The latter, asking almost no questions, might approve a less
than tactful million-dollar campaign contributor as ambassador to another nation; whereas it will peruse the
record, opinions, utterances, and private life of a Supreme Court nominee with great care. Justices, today
especially, are supposed to be the most able, respected,
and wisest of men. It is an act of faith for every elected
or appointed official to carry out the orders of the Supreme Court. All effort to interfere with its nature,
work, or deliberations is instantly and vigorously disap-
proved. Even so popular a president as Franklin Roosevelt was ignobly defeated in 1937 when he sought to
pack the court by adding extra justices.

Such reverence for the court is perhaps inevitable,
considering the powers it has assumed, but it is surely
strange. When its pluses and minuses are tallied, the
court system has had a largely negative effect on American history. That is a rather strong statement and must
be supported with some evidence.

The Constitution says what the Supreme Court inter-
prets it as saying. That is now axiomatic in America.
One of the effects of the judicial veto over legislative
acts and executive decisions has been to greatly increase
the checks and balances which the Founding Fathers
built into the Constitution. The nature of the two houses
of Congress and their relations with the president
make it difficult to form a majority and pass laws. The
judicial veto increases the difficulties by giving to nine
men a review over the constitutionality of those laws.

The additional check and balance simply makes it *more* difficult to form a majority and for that majority to act for the public benefit. Deadlock and drift have been enhanced. Professor Commager is among those who believe the nation would have gotten further using majority rule rather than judicial review.

Frequently in its history the court has been simply obstructionist. To be sure, it often later reversed itself under the pressure of public opinion, but the effect was delay and more delay.

After the Civil War, the Republican majority in Congress, led by Representative Thaddeus Stevens and Senator Charles Sumner, sought to give the Negro full citizenship, full protection of the laws, and equal rights. A variety of legislation was passed to that effect. Congress even went so far as to change the Constitution with the thirteenth, fourteenth, and fifteenth amendments to make the protection of black citizens permanent and to make it extremely difficult to alter what had been accomplished. Surely a majority existed, for the amendments required a two-thirds majority of both Houses of Congress and three-fourths of the states. All of this was allowed to go by the boards by the Supreme Court. The justices could hardly declare a Constitutional amendment unconstitutional, but they upheld a series of state laws which abrogated the amendments and the federal laws. The result of the Court's actions was a century of suffering for blacks and the racial strife that we have today. A negative effect, surely.

The fourteenth amendment, intended to protect minorities, states that no state should "deprive any person of life, liberty, or property without due process of law; nor deny to any person within its jurisdiction the equal protection of the laws." The Supreme Court took that clause and clearly prostituted it by declaring that a *corporation* was a *person*. This emasculated any state efforts to regulate corporations. It made it difficult for any state legislature, or even for Congress, to control the "robber barons," who wasted America's resources, drove competition out of business with unfair practices, and milked the people and the workers while amassing huge profits and achieving great size and strength. At one time or another America's courts struck down nearly every effort of the state or federal governments to improve the lot of workers or to restrain business. The list includes child labor laws, wage and hour laws, safety laws, consumer protection laws.

In the 1930s, the New Deal administration of Franklin Roosevelt sought a massive reform of long-standing business practices, by regulation of business to redistribute the income of Americans, protect labor unions, and control supply and demand for the general economic good. Many of these laws were vetoed by the courts, even though Roosevelt and Congress had huge majorities and a clear mandate from the voters to do what they were doing.

To repeat, the high court later changed its mind on all these matters, as it has on many others, but the effect was long delay and considerable difficulty in getting on with the business of government.

The biggest plus for the Supreme Court in all these years prior to 1950 was in the field of civil rights and individual liberty. Laws seeking to abridge freedom of the press, speech, and assembly were more or less regularly struck down. Court practices which violated a person's right to a fair trial were reversed. Yet even here the same protections were seldom granted to blacks. With this exception, the court enhanced minority rights while remaining a stumbling block to majority rule.

Since the 1950s, the Supreme Court, particularly under Chief Justice Earl Warren, has undergone a massive alteration of its role in government. From 1953 to at least 1970, an activist majority of the high court, ranging from five to nine members, depending upon the issue, has thrust the court into the full fabric of American life. During that tenure it initiated programs as well as vetoed those of other branches of the government.

An activist on the Supreme Court believes that the judiciary is of equal importance in government with the executive and legislative branches. As such it must assume an active role in government to benefit the nation and the people. This, of course, must be done under the law, but the law invades all phases of life. The activist does not change the format of the high court's operations. Cases must still be brought before it by litigants, such as injured parties, those incorrectly accused or convicted, but the Supreme Court has always left unto itself decision as to what cases it wishes to hear. In general the cases have dealt with important constitutional issues, but the Justices decide, in all but rare instances, what is an issue and when they wish to decide it.

There have been many expressions of the activist viewpoint. In 1940, long before the Warren court began, the late Justice Hugo L. Black, one of the foremost activists, wrote in an opinion:

> Under our constitutional system, courts stand against any winds that blow as havens of refuge for those who might otherwise suffer because they are helpless, weak, outnumbered, or because they are nonconforming victims of prejudice and public excitement. . . . No higher duty, no more solemn responsibility, rests upon this Court, than that of translating into living law and maintaining this constitutional shield deliberately planned and inscribed for the benefit of every human being subject to our Constitution — of whatever race, creed or persuasion.[2]

In 1964, Justice William O. Douglas, another activist, rebuked his colleagues for failing to fully decide an important case involving segregation:

> The whole nation has to face the issue; Congress is consistently counseling it; some municipalities have had to make it their first order of concern; law enforcement officers are deeply implicated, North as well as South; the question is at the root of demonstrations, unrest, riots and violence in various areas. The issue in other words commands the public attention. Yet we stand mute, avoiding the decision of the issue by an obvious pretense. . . .
>
> We have in this case a question that is basic to our way of life and fundamental in our constitutional scheme. No question preoccupies the country more than this one; it is plainly justiciable; it presses for decision one way or another; we should resolve it. The people should know that when filibusters occupy other forums, when oppressions are great, when the clash of authority between the individual and the state is severe, they can

still get justice in the courts. When we default, as we do today, the prestige of the law in the life of the nation is weakened.[3]

In opposition, those who believe in judicial restraint argue that the courts should not make law. It is up to those elected by the people — members of legislatures, mayors, governors, presidents — to make law and provide the leadership that leads to laws. If the people wanted laws, they could demand them from those who are elected for this purpose. In the absence of such demand (majority opinion) the courts have no right to force the people to go where they or their representatives do not wish to go. Perhaps the finest expression of judicial restraint came from Justice Felix Frankfurter in 1943. He was dissenting in a case in which the high court (reversing a decision in which Frankfurter had written the majority decision only three years before) voided laws requiring members of the Jehovah's Witness religious sect to salute the flag. Wrote Justice Frankfurter, a Jew:

> One who belongs to the most vilified and persecuted minority in history is not likely to be insensible to the freedoms guaranteed by our Constitution. Were my purely personal attitude relevant, I should wholeheartedly associate myself with the general libertarian views in the court's opinion, representing as they do the thought and action of a lifetime. But as judges we are neither Jew nor Gentile, neither Catholic nor agnostic. We owe equal attachment to the Constitution and are equally bound by our judicial obligations whether we derive our citizenship from the earliest or the latest immigrants to these shores.

> As a member of this court, I am not justified in writing my private notions of policy into the Constitution, no matter how deeply I may cherish them or how mischievous I may deem their disregard. . . . It would require more daring than I possess to deny that reasonable legislators could have taken the action which is before us for review.[4]

The activist majority of the Warren Court ruled in case after case on matters which could have been decided by Congress or state legislators, but which had not been. It ordered racial desegregation of public schools; then determined the speed with which the order should take effect; then, along with lower federal courts, decided specific issues in local school districts, approving or disapproving local plans for school integration. After more than fifteen years had passed, it ordered immediate school desegregation and bussing of children to outlying schools to achieve a form of racial balance which it determined.

Prayers in schools were banned; then any sort of religious exercise. Obscenity was defined, as was what constituted an invasion of privacy.

Among its more far-reaching decisions were those reapportioning Congress and the state legislatures in conformance with the rule of "one man, one vote." Justice Frankfurter had warned about entering this "political thicket," but the court did. The case, *Baker v. Carr*, came from Tennessee which had an extremely mal-apportioned state legislature. Justice Tom Clark expressed a most activist view when the Supreme Court decided that apportionment was a problem for the courts to decide:

. . . I would not consider intervention by this court into so delicate a field if there were any other relief available to the people of Tennessee. But the majority of the people of Tennessee have no practical opportunity for exerting their political weight at the polls to correct the existing "invidious discrimination." Tennessee has no initiative and referendum. I have searched diligently for other "practical opportunities" present under the law. I find none other than through the Federal courts. The majority of the voters have been caught up in a legislative straitjacket. . . . Legislative policy has riveted the present seats in the Assembly to their respective constituencies and by the rates of their incumbents a reapportionment of any kind is prevented. The people have been rebuffed at the hands of the Assembly. They have tried the constitutional convention route, but since the call (for the convention) must originate in the Assembly, it, too, has been fruitless.

They have tried Tennessee courts with the same result, and the Governors have fought the tide only to flounder. It is said that there is recourse in Congress and perhaps that might be, but from a practical standpoint this is without substance. To date Congress has never undertaken such a task in any state. We, therefore, must conclude that the people of Tennessee are stymied and without judicial intervention will be saddled with the present discrimination in the affairs of their state government.[5]

The state legislatures were ordered reapportioned, both in their Senate and lower houses. So was Congress. The courts decided what equal representation was and when it had been achieved.

The Supreme Court was also extremely active in the field of criminal justice, deciding rules of evidence, police procedures in searches and seizures, admissibility of confessions as evidence, how evidence might be obtained, and many other matters. These rulings have had great effect on crime, punishment, and law enforcement throughout the land. Such matters differ from reapportionment or integration problems in that criminal justice seems more within the province of the judiciary system.

Under the reign of the activists, the court has been thrust more and more into fields formerly the sole property of the legislative and executive branches. Members of minorities and even majorities have instituted court actions aimed at achieving social purposes until Supreme Court Justices have had to disclaim the ability to solve all the nation's ills.

Two widely disparate examples may illustrate. Environmentalists, seeking to protect the nation's air, water, and earth, increasingly go to court to obtain orders enforcing laws. Not illogically, such tasks as these could more easily be carried out by elected officials, law enforcers, and regulatory agencies. In its term beginning October 1971, the court has agreed to hear cases on whether the death penalty is legal in the United States. Opponents of the death penalty are hoping for a decision banning it. Is the death penalty not a matter for legislative action? The British Parliament, after long debate, took such action.

Many people admire at least some of the Supreme Court rulings of recent years. (Lest my bias be suspected, let me state that I applaud most of them, particularly desegregation, reapportionment, and protection of individual liberties.) But we might all ponder the words of Justice Frankfurter in his dissent in *Baker v. Carr:*

Such a massive repudiation of the experience of our whole past in asserting destructively novel judicial power demands . . . analysis of the role of this court in our constitutional system.

The Supreme Court is the least democratic of our branches of government. Its members are elected by no one. They are appointed, approved, and then left in independence to serve for life, perhaps well past their intellectual prime, perhaps past their responsiveness to public opinion. Not even the Founding Fathers, who wanted government by the wisest and best of men, had in mind that law should be made by just nine of them. To have law made by nine people is the essence of oligarchy, not democracy.

Furthermore, even those who most like the recent Supreme Court rulings should well remember that the membership of the court changes. It has recently undergone a massive change with President Nixon making four appointments. Those who would rely on the court to correct social ills might do well to remember the court's destructive and disruptive past.

13

Public Opinion

ONE OF THE problems with majority rule is how to discover what the majority opinion is. The "tyranny of the minorities" exists in part because of the difficulty of determining what the majority wants.

There is not *one* majority but innumerable majorities. There is a majority view on farm problems, another on labor problems, and still others on taxation, war, urban affairs, environmental issues, length of skirts, uses of "pot," censorship, prison reform, and anything else that might be named. An interested, knowledgeable American might belong to one majority on religion, a minority on economics, a majority on correcting educational problems, a minority on how to provide better health care.

Moreover, the majority on any issue is extremely flexible. Sudden, dramatic, well-publicized events can change majority thinking overnight. President Johnson witnessed a sudden rise in his popularity, as measured by polls, following his meeting with Soviet Premier Kosygin at Glassboro, New Jersey. President Nixon was informed of a similar change in public attitudes after he announced that he would visit China and after he set forth his new economic policies. The conclusion seems to be that the American people, so used to inaction because of minority rule, react favorably to any display of action by a president and Congress.

How is a majority opinion formed or influenced? It may be said that most Americans desire peace. There are a few manufacturing firms that make money out of war and preparation for it, such as those who make guns, tanks, planes, and other implements of war, but it is now widely believed that more money could be made in peaceful pursuits. As evidence consider the fact that the prices of stocks sold on stock exchanges have tended to drop in recent years whenever an international crisis seemed to threaten war.

Certainly the American people want peace. There is a fear of nuclear holocaust, bombing, the death and maiming of sons and husbands. There is a desire for a more orderly existence, relief of tensions, disarmament so the money spent on armaments can go for more useful purposes.

Assuming that is a fair statement of a majority opinion, how did it come about? In part it originated in the minds of men. Any man can experience fear of a nuclear holocaust, a dislike for military service, weariness with international tensions, exasperation with taxation for military preparedness, longing to have a world without all that. And he can do that whether he is an American, a Russian, or a Chinese.

Such attitudes are greatly influenced by what each person reads and sees and hears. The printed word in the form of newspapers, magazines, and books offers information and opinion about war and peace. Radio, television, sermons, public speeches, and conversations with other people have a similar influence. Scenes of war on television or in movies have a tremendous effect. But such influences can be of wide variety, glorifying war, detesting war, or insisting that preparation for war is necessary to prevent war. This variety of information and opinion will be digested by the interested citizen and lead to his opinion.

An individual opinion might be defined, then, as an emotional reaction based upon the information and opinion which has influenced a person. Public opinion or majority opinion or dominant opinion, as it is variously called, might be said to be the views expressed by the largest group that can agree on any subject.

Public opinion on most issues can be easily influenced. Corporations do this routinely through advertising. To give one example, a rational mind might conclude that the labor involved in brushing the teeth is so slight as not to warrant the expense of an electric toothbrush. Through widespread advertising, the manufacturers of electric toothbrushes apparently convinced large numbers of Americans that the appliance was more effective than manual brushing, leading to better dental care, a whiter smile, love, happiness and, as a result, greater personal wealth.

Governments also do this. For fifty-five years, ever

since the Russian Revolution in 1917, Americans have been told that Communism is an inherent, basic evil, a threat to America. This has been a constant theme which Americans have read, heard, and seen. In two periods, after World Wars I and II, opposition to Communism reached the point of hysteria, with "witchhunts" for suspected Communists, arrests, trials, even executions of offenders. In the late 1940s and early 1950s, such a pogrom, led by the late Senator Joseph McCarthy of Wisconsin, silenced nearly all discussion or study of Communism as an intellectual exercise. University professors were denounced and publicly disgraced, along with diplomats, writers, and other artists.

There have been several repercussions from this incessant campaign to influence public opinion. Effective study of Communism has been reduced. Efforts to make use of any possible good in it were nullified. At various times Communism has become a catchword to describe a variety of evils not associated with the ideology. At times dissenters on such matters as civil rights, poverty, and war have been labeled "Communists." Opposition to Communism has brought wars (Korea and Vietnam), international tensions, military preparedness, absence of peace. The United States has also been put in the position of supporting a large number of dictatorships which had only the virtue of being anti-Communist, notable examples being Spain, Portugal, Greece, South Vietnam, and many nations of South America and Asia. Clearly, our fear of Communism has taken precedence even over our love of liberty.

Some influences on public opinion are greater than others. Government can have tremendous influence.

When the president commandeers television and addresses the nation on a matter of his choosing, he is thrust into a brilliant spotlight. Major attention is also given to members of his cabinet, such as the Secretaries of State and Defense, and prominent members of Congress.

The news media also have tremendous influence. There are between ten and twenty newpapers in America which are considered influential, including the New York *Times*, Washington *Post*, St. Louis *Globe Dispatch*, Baltimore *Sun*, Milwaukee *Journal*, Los Angeles *Times*. The coverage these papers give to the news made by government officials and other sources, as well as their editorial opinions, carry great weight. Television is of immense importance because of the amount of time and coverage it gives to various events. Television has had tremendous impact because it shows action. It can show a large crowd (or a small crowd so it looks large) gathered for some purpose. The immediate effect is to indicate that a significant number of people share an opinion.

The effects of non-governmental sources, such as newspapers, authors, television, and crowds of people cannot be exaggerated. Just prior to the Civil War, the dominant opinion in the North was decidedly in favor of the abolition of slavery. Many factors caused this, but a key one was the influence of one man, William Lloyd Garrison. Through his publication, *The Liberator*, he excoriated slavery and demanded abolition. Public opinion was greatly influenced. The Republican party was founded over the issue. Yet *The Liberator* never had a circulation of more than 3,000.

How can a publication with a circulation of 3,000 have such influence? Because in any endeavor, from decorations for a class party to environmental concerns, only a few people are prime movers. They are concerned, they take action, they convince others, and they do most of the work. Others follow. *The Liberator* reached those few prime movers. They in turn spread the word and eventually influenced the masses.

It is still true today. For good or ill, a relative handful of government officials, newspaper and television reporters, authors, movie producers, and college professors have the power to influence public opinion. In 1965, the dominant opinion in America supported the Johnson administration's policy on the war in Vietnam. Today, polls state that 73 percent of Americans want to withdraw from the war. Opposition to it in Congress is dominant. How did the change occur? Partly through public weariness, but to a greater extent through the efforts of the prime movers in the press, television, and universities who convinced a large number of people of the folly of the fighting.

The formation of public opinion is in large measure dependent upon the prime movers. Senator Joseph McCarthy conducted his witchhunts following World War II because few in government, the press, or universities opposed him. Only when criticism of his methods rose was he censured by the Senate and stopped from his activities. Today there is a growing agitation for prison reform in the United States. It has stemmed from President Nixon, the press, teachers, and authors who have pointed out the self-defeating nature of locking men up in "schools for crime." Sometimes public opinion can be changed by a single individual. President Nixon's economic program in 1971 was greeted with wide enthusiasm, which lessened when George Meany, president of the AFL-CIO, spoke out against it as favoring big business over the wage earner. In only a few days, Congress came to see pitfalls that had not been visible initially.

One more example: when the Pentagon Papers, revealing how America entered the war in Vietnam, were stolen, they were handed to influential newspapers for publication.

Influencing public opinion in the United States can be a science and an art. The giant advertising and public relations businesses have developed for this purpose. As we have seen, politicians feel compelled to invest huge sums of money for advertising and related endeavors.

But public opinion is also influenced by the press, radio, television, and simple observations of people. The civil rights, peace, and environment issues stem largely from these sources and government has been forced to follow. A generation ago, fashion designers in Paris, Rome, London, and New York decreed a new fashion and American women slavishly followed. Today (although it may be a temporary phenomenon) women are rejecting these decrees and wearing whatever they like. The sellers of apparel have had to adjust more to public demand than to the dictates of fashion arbiters. Through their purchases of small foreign cars with unchanged styles, Americans have forced auto makers in Detroit to manufacture similar vehicles.

Clearly, public opinion in America is both more responsive and more individualistic than it was a generation ago. Causes of this change include such factors as the excesses of advertisers; the increased education of Americans (half the high school graduates go to college and the quality of high school education has improved); more mobility, permitting groups of like-minded people to get together at places such as Woodstock; and television's penchant for showing the unusual and the dissenting.

There is danger in all this for the political system. The press and television, by concentrating on a minor phenomenon, can greatly influence public opinion. It is conceivable that by dwelling on something such as the American Nazi party, the press and television could give an exceedingly small minority great influence. The press and television have in recent years given great publicity to hippies, people living in communes, movie stars who marry foreign princes, women who keep children born out of wedlock, abortions, when in fact these are not dominant practices, nor does a large or significant majority engage in them. They are merely bizarre. In 1971, *Time* magazine ran a photograph of a man being married to two women. A person can only imagine the difficulties the magazine must have had in finding such a picture and the need for sensation that dictated its publication.

The need to measure public opinion on any issue has led to the creation of the polling industry. There are a number of companies (George Gallup, Louis Harris are examples) devoted to the task of finding out what Americans think about anything at any given moment.

Americans have a basic distrust of polls. It seems implausible that by questioning a thousand or fifteen hundred people pollsters can predict what 200 million Americans think. This, plus the fact that most Americans have never been questioned by any pollster on any subject, makes the whole process seem ridiculous. Actually, there is a scientific basis to polling. A small number of people, if correctly chosen, can speak for a much larger number. As we have seen, a politician can predict the outcome of an election on the basis of a single key precinct.

The problems of polls are more serious than the method used. The sample questioned must be a true sample. The politican doesn't predict on the basis of *any* precinct, but on one that has very special characteristics, making it typical of the whole election district. The question asked is of crucial importance. If improperly worded, the question can lead the person being interviewed to give a desired answer. Such a question as, "Don't you think the president is doing well in office?" is leading, while asking "Do you approve or disapprove of the president's performance in office?" is less leading. Pollsters are aware of this problem and generally report the question asked as well as statistics about the answer.

The most serious problem with polls is verifying them. Twenty years ago a professor in my college said, "If the people of the world were asked whether the world was round or flat, the flats would win nine to one." He said it as a witticism, knowing full well no one could prove him wrong. A similar situation exists when polls report that X percentage of Americans approve of the president's performance, Y percentage want to end the war in Vietnam, and Z percentage want a cut in taxes. In these, as well as most other matters, there is absolutely no way to prove the polls right or wrong. Thus, people tend to accept the polls they agree with. There is the additional problem that polls may influence other people through the bandwagon effect, thus creating public opinion instead of measuring it.

Distrust of polls stems from those few instances when the polls have been proved wrong. An election provides such opportunities. A famous poll predicted that Alfred Landon would defeat Franklin Roosevelt in 1936 and Roosevelt won by one of the largest majorities in history. In 1948, most polls predicted that Thomas Dewey would defeat Harry Truman, but he didn't. In 1970, American pollsters working in Britain predicted a Labour party victory, but the Conservatives won by a large margin.

Forecasting an election is extremely difficult for pollsters. They admit their results may be in error by from three to five percent. Many elections, such as the presidential elections of 1960 and 1968, were decided by less than one percent. Many pollsters will today say only that an election will be close. An additional problem is that the voter tends to make up his mind or change his mind in the isolation of the voting booth. A Democrat may be thinking of voting Republican; then, alone in the booth, revert for entirely emotional reasons to the pattern of a lifetime.

Despite their faults, polls are valuable. They are one of the few ways we have in America of determining public opinion. They are read by men in government and they do influence them.

14

Using the System

"I think giving the kids the vote is a step forward, but all we can do is vote in an already faulty system."
                                    — POLLY SPIEGEL

I AM ENDING this book, as I began it, with Miss Spiegel's quoted comment, for I believe it to be astute and representative of a prevailing opinion among young people. The effort of this book has been to describe The System, earmark its faults, and list changes that have been suggested.

I would like to suggest that changing the system ought to be in the category of *improving* or *reforming* The System. It may be slow, unresponsive, and frequently undemocratic, but The System has worked for almost two centuries. Americans are generally prosperous.

214

Even the poverty in America is relative. And we have managed to hold on to a high level of the liberty which the Founders so cherished. The times when liberty is impinged should not cause a person to lose sight of the times when it shines like a beacon.

Miss Spiegel's statement that *all* the young people can do is vote in an already faulty system is patently untrue. The System can be *used* to effect change. It is a time-honored art in America and a bit of a science. There are two principal ways to use the system for a desired end. The first is bloc voting.

One of the earliest and surely the most successful practitioners of bloc voting were Irish-Americans. It is largely forgotten today, but the Irish were victims of prejudice. An elderly Irishman can remember signs reading "Irish need not apply" for jobs or housing. The Irish learned rather quickly to use The System by bloc voting. They elected Irishmen to city councils, state legislatures, governorships, as representatives, senators, and finally to the presidency. John F. Kennedy, an Irish-American Catholic, was the first and so far only president who was not a WASP — White Anglo-Saxon Protestant. Italians, Polish, and other ethnic minorities learned to use the same technique. It is of more than passing interest that one of the leading contenders for the Democratic nomination for president, Edmund Muskie, is of Polish-Catholic extraction.

The Irish vote, or the Italian, Polish, or Greek vote is largely a thing of the past in America. Lip service is still given to it, but the ethnic minorities have largely won the goals they set out to achieve. Nevertheless, bloc voting still exists. Although Jews often deny it, their vote is still potent in urban centers. The labor vote is still a factor on specific issues of paramount interest to workingmen.

The most observable example of bloc voting today is the black vote. Since the New Deal administration of Franklin Roosevelt, the Negro vote has been overwhelmingly Democratic, roughly 90 percent. As a result of the sit-in and other civil rights demonstrations of the late 1950s and early 1960s, Negroes won the vote. Various Negro organizations, notably the NAACP, launched an immense campaign to instruct Negroes how to register, how to vote, and how to make that vote most effective.

The results are today quite remarkable. There are black sheriffs, councilmen, legislators, congressmen, mayors. There is one black senator and a member of the race sits on the Supreme Court. At one time, fairly recently, a black sat in the cabinet. Because of the power of the Negro bloc vote, white Southern governors and senators have, to a large extent, ceased their historic race-baiting. Before the black man had the vote, the white Southerner could run on a race-hating program. Today most Southern governors are moderates. They take a clearly conciliatory position toward Negro citizens. Black congressmen in Washington have formed a separate caucus to lobby for housing, welfare, education, and other programs of benefit to black people. A program has been launched to elect black delegates to the Democratic National Convention so that the voting bloc can have greater influence on the nomination.

The Negro was very late in finding the means to use

The System, but a simple perusal of the daily newspaper indicates he is arriving at political power in abundance. By using The System, rather than flailing away at it, he is making gains.

Question: what other group in America has the same potential? There is one. Politicians are waiting for the 1972 elections with the proverbial "bated breath" (whatever that means) to see whether there is such a thing as the youth vote. If young people vote as a bloc, it could have a tremendous effect on American politics.

Analysis of bloc voting shows that the bloc must be segregated and it must be a victim of discrimination. It must have no other recourse to right what it conceives as wrongs. The ethnic minorities were all segregated as is the Negro. They were warrened into ghettos. They had special newspapers and radio stations reaching only the minority. The thinking of the minority could thus be consolidated. It could be reached.

Is this true of American youth? It is segregated. I didn't realize how much until I moved to Spain. The contrast with America is most apparent. The Spanish have an inordinate love for children. Public displays of affection for children are abundant. Kissing of children and fondling of them by parents, grandparents, aunts and uncles, even total strangers is a national custom. To give an example, a bar in Spain is an important social activity for Spanish men. It is quite ordinary for three or four generations of Spanish men to gather in a bar to socialize and play games of dice and dominoes. It is accepted practice for an eighteen-year-old Spaniard, returning from work, to go to the corner bar and greet his father and grandfather with a kiss on the cheek. They have a beer, talk, play a game or two. No one feels alienated. The fathers and grandfathers teach the teenagers how to act in a bar, how to drink a little and enjoy it without becoming drunk. And, presumably, the elders also learn from the youth. The women do not gather in bars, but they have their own methods of mixing the generations.

Americans do not do this—sad to say. The generations seldom mix. Each is deprived of the other. How this came to pass is hard to figure.

Young people in America are segregated into schools, colleges, and universities. The generations meet only in families—and sometimes not even then—and wonder why they misunderstand each other and have little in common. Youth is treated in America like some special condition in life. At some unascertained point a youth becomes an adult, having received little training for that role.

American youth has its own means of communication through high school and college newspapers, music, dress, and much more. Adults don't understand and youth does not want them to. Youth also has tremendous influence. Consider only retail sales. Someone realized that young people have a tremendous amount of money to spend, as much as many billions of dollars a year. It is what is called discretionary income; that is, it doesn't go for housing and food. The money is spent for clothes, records, sports equipment, entertainment, cars, books, and whatever else youth feels like buying. The result is the boutique and other shops aimed at garnering this uncommitted money. America, it is said, is "youth conscious" as a result.

Clearly, the means for a youth vote are all there: segregation, communication, and economic power. The sole question is whether it will be used. Not all such groups have made use of their power. The women's vote never has amounted to much. Oh, politicians pay lip service to it. They organize teas. They appoint an occasional cabinet officer and judge, but no politician is ever very afraid of or, consequently, very influenced by the women's vote. They have never voted as a bloc.

If youth do not vote as a bloc, if they diffuse their vote among many candidates and many issues, their influence in The System will become nil.

To use the system, the youth of America must find a way to unite and form a bloc. Through letters and meetings, articles in the press which youth read, through books (most Americans are unaware that there is a sizeable segment of the publishing industry putting out books for young people, such as this one), youth must find common aspirations.

Several likely goals are at hand. One would be the ending of discriminatory laws and practices. Now that eighteen-year-olds have the vote, it is clearly discriminatory that they cannot hold office. Young people could demand an amendment to the Constitution lowering the age of membership in government. Under the Constitution a person must be twenty-five to be president. Thus, an eighteen-year-old must wait seven years before he can have any direct role in national affairs. It would be truly remarkable if young people did not begin to demand a change in the Constitution.

Other laws and state constitutions restrict the age of state and local officeholders. It could certainly be argued that eighteen-year-olds, being closer to their education, have the knowledge and wisdom to participate in governmental affairs. Youth could easily war against discriminatory insurance rates for youthful drivers. They could denounce discriminatory police practices whereby police arrest offenders on the basis of age or haircuts. Indeed, the law books are larded with laws which discriminate against youth.

Obviously, there are several matters in America which are the natural concern of youth because they are the ones overwhelmingly affected. These include education, the juvenile court system, police juvenile departments, juvenile correctional institutions, selective service, military training of inductees, child guidance centers, youth training programs, youth unemployment, and many others. Equally obviously, youth could argue that it has a legal right to participate in decisions involving war and peace, pollution, over-population, housing, welfare, urban problems, and other issues, for the decisions made today affect the world youth will inherit. Youth can argue that it has the knowledge, wisdom, and concern to participate in decisions on these matters and that it is patently discriminatory for adults to decide these matters *for* youth but without participation *by* youth.

To use the system for these ends, youth must demonstrate that its vote is powerful. It must demonstrate to professional politicians that certain candidates won or lost because the youth vote was granted or withheld. It must be a statistical certainty. Eventually, youth must begin to nominate and elect people who represent its views. The secret to this is to seek victory. The key is local politics. If a teenager ran for president or governor or senator, he would be doomed to failure, even if there were no age restrictions. But it is eminently possible to elect a youthful sheriff, city councilman, board of education member, state legislator, or delegate to a national convention. Minor local offices have power in themselves, but they also demonstrate that youth can serve the nation well. There is virtue in having a teenage sheriff, city councilman, school board member, or national convention delegate. They have something to contribute and can perform well, perhaps better than their elders. Eventually, there will be a twenty-year-old mayor and his or her city will prosper; eventually, also, if there are enough of them, young people will have a strong voice in the nomination of a president.

Eventually! It has already happened! After the above was written, Ron Hooker, a 19-year-old junior at Ashland College, was elected mayor of Newcomerstown, Ohio. He is believed to be the youngest mayor in the nation and perhaps the youngest ever. He ran as an independent, write-in candidate against a former mayor on a pledge to stop "hot-rodding and speeding." He won by a landslide 3-1 margin in the town of 4,500. The election produced the largest voter turnout in a mayoralty race in the town's history. A number of other teenagers ran for public office in November 1971, including Miss Yvonne Westbrook, 18, of San Francisco, seeking the office of county supervisor; Walter Sobol, 18, who was narrowly defeated for city council in Richland, Washington; and David Lambert, who ran for the school board in Bexley, Ohio. Clearly young candidates are beginning to make political waves.

One more ingredient is vital. Youth must temper its

idealism and energy with sagacity. Compromise is the essence of The System. The voting bloc seeks and wins the support of other blocs. If it cannot gain *all* it wants, it accepts a little. A youth bloc might form alliances with environmentalists, for example, or with the blacks, or with the elderly. Youth might, for example, support an anti-pollution program or an improved health plan for the aged in return for support by the conservationists or the elderly for an educational program. Such compromise *is* The System. By such compromise is The System used.

Youth, to use The System, does not need a formal organization. There need be no National Youth Council (or whatever) to speak for young people as the AFL-CIO does for labor or the NAACP and other organizations for blacks. There can be a variety of organizations or none at all, as long as there is communication between high school and college campuses.

All the circumstances for youth bloc voting exist. Youth are gathered in colleges and high schools. They are discriminated against and have genuine grievances. The means of communication between the separate campuses exist. All that is needed is the will and the know-how to use The System so as to appeal to youth, to develop a program—if only one of electing youthful officeholders—to call for voter registration programs, and to call for bloc voting.

The second method of using the system may be summarized in one name, Ralph Nader. Whether you agree with him or not, he has learned while still in his thirties to use The System. A lawyer by training, he began with the printed word, a book, *Unsafe At Any Speed*, to denounce the rear end suspension system of the Corvair automobile. He was a David taking on a Goliath, the largest industrial corporation in America, General Motors. Ultimately, he forced the Corvair off the market. The nation's concern for automobile safety and environmental controls can be traced in large measure to this single individual.

He is credited with passage of the National Traffic and Motor Vehicle Safety Act, the Wholesome Meat Act, the Natural Gas Pipeline Safety Act, the Radiation Control for Health and Safety Act, and the Wholesale Poultry Products Act. The Interstate Commerce Commission and the Federal Trade Commission are among the federal agencies which Nader has discovered to be moribund, inefficient, and corrupt. Banks, stores, whole industries, even the State of California have come under his scrutiny and been accused of faults, both gross and small.

Nader's methods are well known. He announces an investigation, even receiving the cooperation of the company or agency to be investigated. He turns loose a group of young, able, intelligent investigators called "Nader's Raiders." They make on-the-spot studies and issue a factual report. Nader abhors rhetoric and deals solely in facts, presenting both sides of a question when two sides exist. He has won respect for his factualness and his fairness, as well as his absence of personal self-interest. He is a self-proclaimed representative of the public and the consumer.

Nader is on a first-name basis with key members of

Congress. He lobbies for the public interest; that is, he provides information which enables congressmen to do what Nader believes will benefit the public. He is untiring in this. He continually barrages key members of Congress with information and opinion. Similar actions are taken with members of the bureaucracy.

A youth special interest group could do the same. Rather than blowing up buildings, staging strikes, and demanding a change in The System, youth might use The System. On a matter such as education, youth groups known to represent students might be far more effective if they talked to members of the Office of Education and the House and Senate Education Committees, providing them with information to lead them toward a desired course. Similar actions could be taken in such matters as pollution, selective service, laws discriminatory against age, and other matters of special concern to youth.

It might be argued that The System just ought to work automatically. The federal government ought to realize what young people want and need and do it. But this is pie-in-the-sky. We are a government of special interests, whether we ought to be that way or not. The point is that the best, quickest, and surest way to get the government moving is to use The System through voting blocs and lobbying. It takes effort and know-how. But it works. That has been proven time and again. I hope the youth of America will try.

Notes

CHAPTER ONE
1 "How Will the Young Vote?", *Time*, August 23, 1971, p. 24.

CHAPTER TWO
1 In a book of that title, *The Territorial Imperative* by Robert Ardrey, Atheneum, New York, 1966; and Delta paperback, Dell Publishing Co., New York, 1966.

CHAPTER THREE
1 From Jefferson's letter to Samuel Kercheval of July 1816. Quoted by Henry Steele Commager in *Majority Rule and Minority Rights*, Oxford University Press, New York, 1943. Also quoted by Hillman M. Bishop and Samuel Hendel, editors, *Basic Issues of American Democracy*, sixth edition, Appleton-Century-Crofts, New York, 1970.

2 Commager

3 As quoted in Catherine Drinker Bowen's *Miracle at Philadelphia*, Bantam edition, p. 58, Bantam Books, New York.

4   James MacGregor Burns, *The Deadlock of Democracy*, Prentice Hall, Inc., Englewood Cliffs, N. J., 1963, Quoted in Bishop and Hendel.

5   Commager

6   Burns

7   Burns

CHAPTER FOUR

1   Samuel Eliot Morison, *The Oxford History of the American People*, Oxford University Press, New York, 1965.

2   Quoted by Morison.

CHAPTER FIVE

1   For a fuller discussion of both political organizations and campaign techniques see the author's *Politics From Precinct to President*, Delacorte Press, New York, 1968. It also includes discussion of the modern political boss and modern techniques of graft and soliciting campaign contributions.

2   In my opinion the best single book ever written on local party politics was Frank R. Kent's *The Great Game of Politics*, published in 1923 by Doubleday, Page & Co., Garden City, N.Y. Understandably, Kent's examples are now dated, but his exposition of how local politics works remains highly valid.

CHAPTER SIX

1   In 1972, the Democratic party will have moved perilously close to this system. About two-thirds of the delegates to the National Convention will have been chosen in primaries in twenty-two states, including several large ones. If one man receives the bulk of the delegates through the primaries he is nearly assured of election. Only if several candidates win important primaries will the convention kingmakers have a chance to influence the nomination. It is also anticipated that the convention will have a major argument over the seating of various elected delegates. The reliance on primaries has been cited as more democratic, yet the abuses already cited above are clearly apparent.

2   Of necessity I have made only a general presentation of

the new rules for selection of convention delegates. They are simply too voluminous to be detailed in a work of this kind. For more specific information, including how individual party members may participate in the delegate-selection process and even become delegates, contact the Democratic National Committee, 2600 Virginia Avenue, N.W., Washington, D.C. 20037 or the Dwight D. Eisenhower Republican Center, 310 First Street, S.E., Washington, D.C. 20003.

3   It is largely forgotten today, but Washington left office roundly denounced by his critics. This is perhaps another tradition established by Washington—for presidents to be unpopular when they leave office, but to be admired later. In modern times it happened to Herbert Hoover and Harry Truman. Lyndon Johnson, now a retired president, is perhaps looking forward to a similar development in time.

CHAPTER SEVEN

1   Joe McGinniss, *The Selling of the President 1968*, Trident Press, New York, 1969.

2   McGinniss. This quote came from the Pocket Book edition, pp. 103-4.

3   "The High Cost of Democracy," *Time*, November 23, 1970, p. 13.

4   "The Ticklish Problem of Political Fund-Raising," *The Reader's Digest*, January 1968, pp. 64-69.

CHAPTER EIGHT

1   For a fuller discussion of Mr. Mills and his unique power, read *Power in Washington* by Douglass Cater. Random House, New York, 1964. Also available in a Vintage paperback.

2   The historic vote for British entry into the European Common Market in November 1971 illustrates another key difference between Congress and the House of Commons. Public opinion polls had shown a small majority of the British people opposed to entry, while an overwhelming majority believed Britain would enter. This paradox reflects the long constitutional tradition in Britain that issues are decided by Parliament, not by popular referendum. In the tradition of

Edmund Burke, the great eighteenth-century Conservative, members of Parliament are expected to act wisely for the benefit of the nation and not follow slavishly the views of constitutents.

3   *The Legislative Process in Congress* by George Galloway, Thomas Y. Crowell, New York, 1953. Quoted by Cater.

4   J. S. Clark, *Congress: The Sapless Branch*, revised paperback edition, Harper & Row, New York, 1964.

CHAPTER NINE

1   Senate Foreign Relations Committee report on Security Agreements and Commitments Abroad. Available from Government Printing Office, Washington, D.C.

2   For a fuller treatment of both the Symington report and the entire problem of presidential powers read the author's *Presidential Power: How Much is Too Much?* McGraw-Hill, New York, 1971.

3   Congress is most effective, many contend, as an investigative body, as the Symington report illustrates. Congressional committees have the power to call witnesses, elicit expert testimony, and issue reports, which are often extremely effective in spotlighting national problems. Such hearings are often particularly effective because Senators and Representatives, some of whom are quite knowledgeable about particular matters, are able to question the expert witnesses. Many political scientists have urged that the investigative function of Congress be enhanced by the expenditure of more funds for this purpose, and for the enlargement of investigative staffs to make the investigations of national problems and government operations more permanent, consistent, and thorough.

4   For my discussion of the Pentagon Papers I have relied upon the New York *Times* version as reprinted in the *International Herald Tribune*, Paris, France.

CHAPTER TEN

1   Published by John Wiley & Son, New York, 1960. Also available in a Wiley paperback.

2   A number of political scientists now believe that the twenty-second amendment to the Constitution was a mistake

and should be repealed. It limits presidents to two terms. At the time of its proposal in 1951, it was argued that during his second term a president would not have to play politics and could courageously do what was best for the country. But politics being politics, it has turned out that presidents noticeably lose effectiveness when it is known they will not or cannot run again. The floodgates of politics are opened and members of Congress and the bureaucracy feel less need to heed a man who simply isn't going to be around very long.

CHAPTER ELEVEN

1   Published by Random House, New York, 1970.

2   John Kenneth Galbraith, *The New Industrial State*, Houghton Mifflin Co., Boston, 1967. Also in a Signet paperback.

3   Mills discussed his thesis in two books, *The Power Elite*, Oxford University Press, New York, 1956, and *Power, Politics and People: The Collected Essays of C. Wright Mills*, which was also published by Oxford in 1963. I made use of Bishop and Hendel, *op. cit*, pp. 503-17.

4   Walter Lippmann, *The Phantom Public*, The Macmillan Co., New York, 1927.

CHAPTER TWELVE

1   Marbury v. Madison (1 Cranch 137)

2   Chambers v. Florida (309 U.S. 227)

3   Bell v. Maryland (378 U. S. 226)

4   West Virginia State Board of Education v. Barnette (319 U. S. 624)

5   Baker v. Carr (369 U. S. 186)

Selected Reading

Bishop, Hillman M. and Hendel, Samuel, editors; *Basic Issues of American Democracy*, sixth edition; Appleton-Century-Crofts, New York, 1970.

Boorstin, Daniel J.; *The Americans: The National Experience;* Random House, New York, 1965.

Bowen, Catherine Drinker; *Miracle at Philadelphia;* Little, Brown and Co., Boston, 1966.

Burns, James MacGregor; *The Deadlock of Democracy;* Prentice-Hall, Inc., Englewood Cliffs, N.J., 1963.

Cater, Douglass; *Power in Washington;* Random House, New York, 1964.

Clark, Joseph S.; *Congress: The Sapless Branch;* Harper & Row, New York, 1964.

Commager, Henry Steele; *Majority Rule and Minority Rights;* Oxford University Press, New York, 1943.

Davidson, Roger H.; *The Role of The Congressman;* Pegasus, New York, 1969.

Degler, Carl N.; *Out of Our Past;* Harper & Row, New York, 1970.

Galbraith, John Kenneth; *The New Industrial State;* Houghton Mifflin Co., Boston, 1967.

Galloway, George; *The Legislative Process in Congress;* T. Y. Crowell, New York, 1953.

James, Dorothy Buckton; *The Contemporary Presidency;* Pegasus, New York, 1969.

Laski, Harold J.; *The American Presidency;* Grosset & Dunlap, New York, 1940.

Lewis, Anthony; *Gideon's Trumpet;* Random House, New York, 1964.

Liston, Robert A.; *Politics from Precinct to President;* Delacorte Press, New York, 1968.

Liston, Robert A.; *Tides of Justice;* Delacorte Press, New York, 1966.

Masters, Nicholas A., and Baluss, Mary E.; *The Growing Powers of the Presidency;* Parents' Magazine Press, New York, 1968.

McGinniss, Joe; *The Selling of the President, 1968;* Trident Press, New York, 1969.

Morison, Samuel Eliot; *The Oxford History of the American People;* Oxford University Press, New York, 1965.

Neustadt, Richard E.; *Presidential Power: The Politics of Leadership;* John Wiley & Son, New York, 1960.

Rossiter, Clinton; *The American Presidency;* Harcourt, Brace and World, New York, 1956.

Walton, Richard J.; *Beyond Diplomacy;* Parents' Magazine Press, New York, 1970.

Index